AN UNOFFICIAL ENCYCLOPEDIA OF STRATEGY FOR FORTNITERS

ATK DRIVING TECHNIQUES, CHALLENGES, AND STUNTS

AN UNOFFICIAL ENCYCLOPEDIA OF STRATEGY FOR FORTNITERS

ATK DRIVING TECHNIQUES, CHALLENGES, AND STUNTS

JASON R. RICH

Sky Pony Press
New York

Copyright © 2018 by Hollan Publishing, Inc.

Fortnite ® is a registered trademark of Epic Games, Inc.

The *Fortnite* game is copyright © Epic Games, Inc.

Sky Pony Press books may be purchased in bulk at special discounts for sales promotion, corporate gifts, fund-raising, or educational purposes. Special editions can also be created to specifications. For details, contact the Special Sales Department, Sky Pony Press, 307 West 36th Street, 11th Floor, New York, NY 10018 or info@ skyhorsepublishing.com.

Sky Pony® is a registered trademark of Skyhorse Publishing, Inc.®, a Delaware corporation.

Visit our website at www.skyponypress.com.

Authors, books, and more at SkyPonyPressBlog.com.

10 9 8 7 6 5 4 3 2 1

Library of Congress Cataloging-in-Publication Data is available on file.

Series design by Brian Peterson

Print ISBN: 978-1-5107-4455-4
Ebook ISBN: 978-1-5107-4463-9

Printed in China

TABLE OF CONTENTS

AN UNOFFICIAL ENCYCLOPEDIA OF STRATEGY FOR FORTNITERS

ATK DRIVING TECHNIQUES, CHALLENGES, AND STUNTS

SECTION 1

WELCOME TO THE ISLAND!

What do more than 125 million gamers from all over the world have in common? Well, they probably all enjoy eating pizza, but they also love playing *Fortnite: Battle Royale*. This fast-action, ultra-intense, combat adventure can be experienced on a PC, Mac, PlayStation 4, Xbox One, Nintendo Switch, Apple iPhone, Apple iPad, or an Android-based mobile device.

An Overview of *Fortnite: Battle Royale*

Whichever gaming system you use, when you play *Fortnite: Battle Royale*, you take on the role of a soldier who gets transported to a mysterious island that's filled with many different locations to explore. As you'll soon discover, each offers unique terrain and a different collection of challenges.

To make your stay on the island even more difficult, within moments after you land, a dangerous storm forms and begins to expand and move across the island, making the land uninhabitable. You'll need to avoid the storm! The areas of the island map displayed in pink have already been ravaged by the storm. However, avoiding the storm is not your only challenge—far from it!

At the same time you're transported to the island (via a flying blue bus, called the Battle Bus), up to 99 other soldiers, each controlled in real-time by a different gamer, also get transported to the mysterious island. These are your adversaries.

From the Lobby, after choosing a game play mode and selecting the Play option, a match will begin. You'll be transported to the pre-deployment area (shown here). This is where you'll wait until up to 99 other gamers join the match. Your soldier will board the flying Battle Bus, which transports all of the soldiers (allies and enemies alike) to the island.

To ensure a safe landing, engage your soldier's glider at any time. This slows down their rate of descent and gives you more precise navigational control.

As the Battle Bus flies over the island, choose a desired landing location and then help your soldier leap from the bus to begin a freefall toward land. Use your controller to navigate as your soldier falls. To increase their falling speed and reach land faster, point your soldier downward.

Once your soldier lands on the island, he or she is armed only with their trusty pickaxe. It's now your responsibility to move to a safe location and start collecting weapons, ammo, loot items, and resources in order to build up your arsenal. Ideally, you want to grab at least one weapon (and some ammo) before you encounter an enemy soldier and engage in your first firefight or battle.

Your primary objective from this moment forward is to defeat your enemies and become the last person alive at the end of the match, so that you achieve #1 Victory Royale. There is no second or third place. Either you become the last person standing, or you're eliminated from the match.

Discover What You Can Do from the Lobby

Each time you launch *Fortnite: Battle Royale* on your gaming system, you'll find yourself in the Lobby. From here, you can access the game's menu to customize settings, choose your game play mode, or access one of the command tabs displayed along the top of the screen. These are labeled Lobby (shown above), Battle Pass, Challenges, Locker, Item Shop, and Store.

Choose the Battle Pass option to purchase a *Fortnite: Battle Royale* Battle Pass. This is a collection of approximately 100 tiers, each of which offers one or more challenges that you can complete in order to unlock prizes. Each Battle Pass lasts for one gaming season (approximately three months). When a new season of *Fortnite: Battle Royale* begins, a new Battle Pass is offered by Epic Games, and the older Battle Pass expires. From this screen, you can purchase a Battle Pass, plus see what prizes will be unlocked each time you complete a tier-based challenge.

Once you purchase a Battle Pass, which is optional, return to this screen to purchase and unlock one (optional) Battle Pass tier at a time. Do this if you want to receive the prize offered for a particular tier, without first completing the challenges.

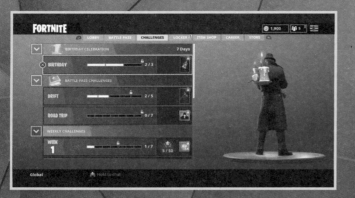

From the Lobby, select the Challenges tab to view and participate in the daily, weekly, and special challenges offered by Epic Games. A Battle Pass is not required for these free challenges, but the prizes you can win are not as rare or exciting as the prizes offered if you've purchased an optional Battle Pass.

From the Locker, select the Outfit slot and choose from the outfits you've already unlocked, acquired, or won. Outfits are the clothing your soldier wears.

Purchased items from the Item Shop, acquired free items, or unlocked items won by completing challenges are all collected and stored within the Locker. Items are used to customize the appearance of your soldier. There are several different customizations you can make to change what your soldier looks like.

Each day, Epic Games releases new outfits. Some are considered "legendary" and very rare. They're only available for a short time. It's been over one year since *Fortnite: Battle Royale* was first released, and hundreds of optional outfits have already been made available.

Along with each outfit, choose an optional back bling design. This is what your soldier's backpack will look like. In some cases, once you select an outfit from the Item Shop, matching back bling comes bundled with it, although this is considered a separate item. On the left side of the screen, you can see the "legendary" Moisty Merman outfit and back bling design that's about to be purchased together for 2,000 V-Bucks.

Gamers also have the ability to choose a soldier's glider. This is the device used during a soldier's initial freefall after leaping from the Battle Bus to ensure a safe landing on the island. The glider is also used when a soldier steps through a Rift, uses a Rift-to-Go, or after jumping on a Launch Pad, for example. Again, there are many optional glider designs available, but they all function exactly the same way.

Next, choose your character's pickaxe design. This is the tool your soldier carries around throughout the entire match. It's used as a close-range weapon, as well as a tool for harvesting resources (wood, stone, and metal), and to smash and destroy objects that get in your way or that need to be removed. While there are many optional pickaxe designs to choose from, they all function exactly the same way.

As your soldier is freefalling from the Battle Bus through the air and traveling toward the ground, a contrail design is the animation you'll see shooting from your soldier's hands. This too is optional. Contrail designs need to be unlocked by completing Battle Pass challenges, completing free challenges, or by downloading free Twitch Prime Packs, for example. They're not typically for sale from the Item Shop. To learn more about Twitch Prime Packs, visit: www.twitch.tv/prime.

From the Locker, before each match, select up to six different emotes that you'll be able to use during a match to showcase your soldier's personality and attitude. There are three types of emotes—graphic icons, spray paint tags, and dance moves.

Each soldier has their own can of virtual spray paint, which he or she can use to create graffiti on any flat surface. To do this, you'll first need to unlock individual spray paint tags. Then choose your favorites and add them, one at a time, to one of the six emote slots in the Locker.

You'll discover many different graphic icons that can be unlocked by completing challenges, for example. When you select one, your soldier will toss it into the air for everyone else in the area to see during a match (or while in the pre-deployment area).

You're able to spray paint one tag at a time while visiting the island.

Once you've unlocked multiple spray paint tags, apply several of them in unique patterns on flat surfaces to create totally lit graffiti designs.

One of the most popular ways for soldiers to express themselves on the island is to perform dance moves. You can unlock or purchase many different dance moves and perform one at a time, or perform several different dance moves in quick succession to show off some complex and attention-getting choreography.

Most outfits cost between 800 and 2,000 V-Bucks, which translates to between $8.00 (US) and $20.00 (US). Some outfits come with a matching back bling design. However, a matching pickaxe design and glider design, when offered, is sold separately. Individual pickaxe designs and glider designs cost between 500 and 1,500 V-Bucks, while each emote costs between 200 and 500 V-Bucks. Shown here is the optional Death Valley pickaxe design being sold from the Item Shop for a whopping 1,500 V-Bucks. (That's about $15.00 US.)

Examples of Popular Soldier Outfits

Some gamers perform dance moves as a greeting while in the pre-deployment area, or as a way to gloat after defeating an enemy. To do this, access this Emotes menu and select one of the six emotes that you want to use.

Keep in mind, all items purchased from the Item Shop are for appearance purposes only. All are optional, and none provide your soldier with any competitive advantage whatsoever. They do, however, allow you to customize the appearance of your soldier, which most gamers agree is pretty awesome.

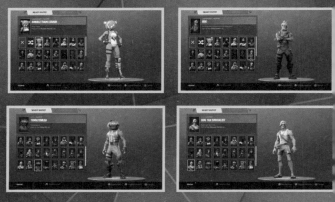

From the Item Shop, when you click on a featured outfit to get a close-up look at it, you'll see that, like weapons and loot items, outfits are categorized as well. A "legendary" outfit is limited edition and only available for a short time, while an Epic or Rare outfit, for example, may periodically re-appear within the Item Shop every few weeks or months. Shown here is the "legendary" Chomp Sr. outfit. As you can see, it showcases a whimsical shark theme.

Keep in mind, certain outfits can only be unlocked by completing Battle Pass challenges, while others are exclusive to gamers who download the promotional Twitch Prime Packs (which are released every few months).

Some outfits, like Raven, Oblivion, and Omen make a soldier look mysterious or sinister, which is sure to strike fear into enemies.

Here are some examples of "legendary," limited-edition outfits that have been released by Epic Games in the past. These include Sky Stalker, Drift, Flytrap, and Red Knight.

To cater to gamers with a sense of humor, Epic Games offers many humorous and ridiculous-looking outfits, such as Cuddle Team Leader, Rex, Tomatohead, and Sun Tan Specialist. Some outfits are released in conjunction with an event happening within the game, while others tie into a real-life holiday or event (such as Christmas, July 4th, or the World Cup Soccer Tournament).

From the Lobby, select the Store option to purchase V-Bucks using real money. The larger the bundle of V-Bucks you purchase at once, the bigger discount you'll receive when purchasing items from the Item Shop. Purchase 600 V-Bucks (as part of the Starter Pack) for $4.99 (US). A bundle of 1,000 V-Bucks costs $9.99 (US). You can save money by purchasing 2,800 V-Bucks for $24.99 (US), 7,500 V-Bucks for $59.99 (US), or 13,500 V-Bucks for $99.99 (US).

Using items you've already purchased from the Item Shop, unlocked, or acquired before a match, visit the Locker to fully customize your soldier. Once this is done, return to the Lobby to choose which *Fortnite: Battle Royale* game play mode you want to experience, and then select the Play option to begin a match. Most individual matches last about 15 minutes, or however long it takes for all of the soldiers on the island to be eliminated, except for just one.

At least once or twice per gaming season, Epic Games offers a Starter Pack from the Store (not the Item Shop). For $4.99 US, you receive an exclusive outfit (which may or may not include accessory items), along with 600 V-Bucks. Shown above, on the left side of the Store screen is a Starter Pack that was offered during Season 5.

Once you've acquired a bunch of outfits, pickaxe designs, and back bling designs, mix and match them from the Locker to give your soldier a truly unique appearance. Of course, you can also stick with the matching outfit, pickaxe design, and back bling design that were released by Epic Games as a matching or theme-oriented set.

Choose a Game Play Mode

From the Choose Game Mode screen, select a game play mode. The three permanent options include: Solo, Duos, and Squads. On an ongoing basis, Epic Games also offers additional, but temporary game play modes, like Playground, and some type of 50 v 50 game play mode. Solo mode allows your soldier to land on the island along with 99 other soldiers. Your soldier must become the last person standing at the end of the match to win #1 Victory Royale.

When you select Duos mode, you and a partner (either an online friend or a random player) can work together as you strive to outlive up to 98 other soldiers during each match.

The Squads game play mode allows you to team up with up to three online friends or random players to create a squad. The four of you will work together, as you battle against other four-soldier squads and attempt to defeat them all.

Playground mode is periodically offered. It gives you 55 minutes to visit and explore the island, build up an arsenal, practice using weapons, collect resources, practice building, and experience mock firefights against online friends or random gamers. Playground mode offers the ideal place to practice and improve your exploration, survival, fighting, and building skills, without the threat of enemy soldiers attacking you, or having to outrun the storm to stay alive.

A 50 v 50 match is another game play mode that's often, but not always, available. This game play mode is unlike all others. It creates two teams comprised of 50 soldiers each, and the island is divided in half. The goal is to defeat the opposing team and to work together with your own teammates to win firefights and battles that many soldiers participate in simultaneously.

Customize *Fortnite: Battle Royale's* Settings and Options

In addition to choosing the appearance of your solider, as a gamer, you can also tweak a wide range of game-related settings to better adapt *Fortnite: Battle Royale* to your personal gaming style and skill level.

If you're a noob, with the exception of the Audio-related options, leave the rest of the default settings intact until you've spent time playing

Fortnite: Battle Royale and determine which features and functions you want to adjust.

To adjust the game's various settings, access the game's menu from the Lobby (shown above). On a PS4, press the Options button on the controller, or on a Nintendo Switch, press the "+" on the controller, for example. Next, select and access the gear-shaped Settings icon. The main game menu and Settings icon appear near the top-right corner of the screen.

Sound effects play an important role in *Fortnite: Battle Royale*. From the Audio sub-menu (shown above), turn down the Music volume, but turn up the Sound FX volume. If you're using a gaming headset with a built-in microphone, you'll be able to speak with your partner or squad members if you turn on and adjust the volume of the Voice Chat feature.

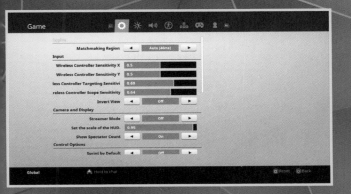

Displayed along the top of the Game Settings menu (shown here on a PS4) are additional icons that give you access to a handful of sub-menus. They're labeled Game (shown here), Brightness, Audio, Accessibility, Controller, and Account. If you're playing on a PC or Mac, instead of a Controller menu option, you'll see an Input option that allows you to assign keyboard keys and mouse buttons to specific game-related features and functions.

If you're playing on a console-based system (PS4, Xbox One, or Nintendo Switch), you'll discover that *Fortnite: Battle Royale* offers four different controller layouts. The default option (shown here on a PS4) is called Old School.

The Quick Builder controller layout is better suited for people who enjoy building, as opposed to focusing on firefights and combat.

For gamers who put a lot of emphasis on building extremely fast when playing *Fortnite: Battle Royale*, choose the Builder Pro controller layout.

If your primary strategy is to participate in firefights during each mission, you may discover that the Combat Pro controller layout (shown here on a PS4) is better suited to your gaming

style. Similar controller layouts are offered when playing the Xbox One or Nintendo Switch version of the game.

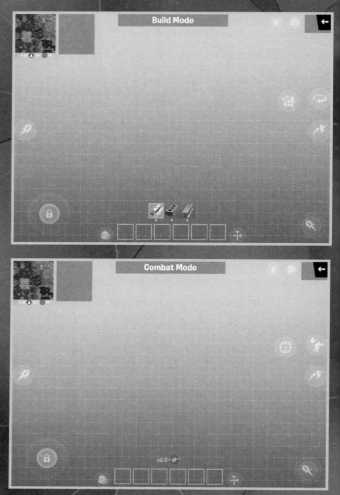

Mobile device users should use the game's HUD Layout Tool to customize the size and location of where the control icons are displayed on the game screen. Separate options are available for Build mode and Combat mode. In addition to customizing these options, access the game's Settings menus, which include Video, Game, Audio, and Account.

Let's Take an Island Tour Aboard an All Terrain Kart (ATK)

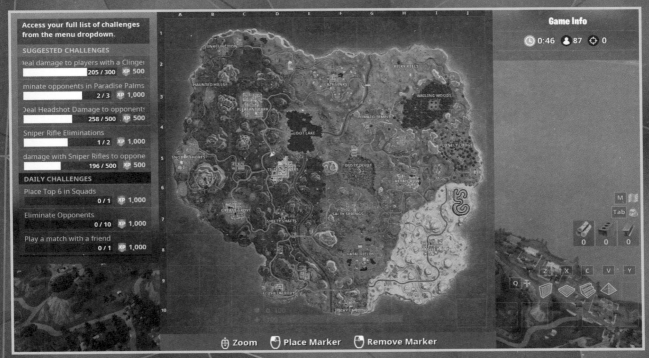

The island where each match takes place has more than 20 points of interest labeled on the island map, as well as many unlabeled areas that are well worth exploring.

One of the most exciting and fun ways to travel around the island was introduced at the start of Season 5. These souped-up golf carts are called All Terrain Karts (ATKs). Depending on which game play mode you're experiencing, between one and four soldiers can ride in an ATK at the same time.

Sure, you can drive an ATK along paved roads on the island to get from one place to another, but the real fun and challenge begins when you take these vehicles off-roading. (Shown here on an iPad Pro.)

Another gaming element added to *Fortnite: Battle Royale* at the start of Season 5 was the random appearance of Rifts. When a soldier walks into a Rift, he or she gets catapulted into the air, and can use their glider to land safely. While in the air, use the directional controls to navigate and help determine a landing location. After it's used, most Rifts disappear. In addition to walking into a Rift, if you're in an ATK, try driving directly into one. Rifts offer yet another way to travel around the island. A Rift-to-Go is a loot item that can be found, collected, and stored in your soldier's backpack until it's needed. It can then be activated anywhere and anytime you want, and it works just like a Rift.

To help you discover what to expect on the mysterious island where each match takes place, Section 3—An "A to Z" Island Tour and Survival Guide offers a preview of each point of interest and provides tips and strategies for surviving within each unique area, based on the type of terrain you'll encounter within each.

Take Full Advantage of Loot Items

In addition to a vast and ever-expanding collection of guns that are available within *Fortnite: Battle Royale*, you'll have the opportunity during each match to find, collect, and use an assortment of loot items.

Loot items can be found within chests, Supply Drops, and Loot Llamas. They're also found lying on the ground, out in the open. Some Vending Machines that are scattered throughout the island sell loot items. When they're available, you can use wood, stone, or metal resources to purchase them. Plus, anytime you defeat an enemy, you're able to collect whatever loot items that soldier was carrying.

There are three types of loot items available during a match. These include:

- Items that can be used as a weapon, such as a Trap, Grenade, Remote Explosives, Stink Bomb, Clingers, Boogie Bombs, Impulse Grenades, and Shockwave Grenades.
- Powerup items that can be used to replenish your soldier's Health meter and/or Shield meter. These include: Bandages, Small Shield Potions, Mushrooms, Med Kits, Shield Potions, Slurp Juice, Chug Jugs, and Cozy Camp Fires.
- Items that can be used as tools to help your soldier survive or move around on the island. These include: Bushes, Launch Pads, Bouncer Pads, a Rift-To-Go, a Port-A-Fort, a Port-A-Fortress, or a Grappler.

Keep in mind, the driver of an ATK can't use a weapon or loot item while actually driving the vehicle. However, passengers of an ATK *can* use any of their weapons or loot items. So, while riding in an ATK as a passenger, if you don't anticipate any incoming attacks, consider using or consuming loot items to replenish your soldier's Health or Shields, for example. If you do come across enemies as a passenger, your soldier can toss Grenades or Clingers at them.

Using a Med Kit will replenish your soldier's Health meter back up to 100. The item takes 10 seconds to use, during which time your soldier can't use a weapon, build, or move. Bandages, however, take only 4 seconds to use, but they only increase a soldier's Health meter by 15 points each.

Finding, grabbing, and then consuming a Chug Jug requires 15 seconds, but once it's been fully consumed, your soldier's Health and Shield meter will be replenished back to 100. These items are rare, so save them for the End Game, when they're most likely to be needed to ensure your survival.

A Port-a-Fortress is a souped-up and larger version of a Port-a-Fort, but very rare.

Once activated, you're able to instantly build a mega-fortress, complete with built-in Traps and Bouncer Pads on the outside walls. A Port-a-Fortress requires no resources to build. It's particularly useful when playing a Duos or Squads match, when multiple soldiers will be using the fortress at the same time.

As you'll discover, there's plenty of room. However, you definitely want to use the same strategies as you'd use when hiding in a Port-a-Fort when it comes to protecting the structure. For example, once you're at the top of a Port-a-Fortress, build a metal floor tile in the center to keep enemies from entering the fortress and following you up to the top.

A Rift-to-Go works like a regular Rift that was introduced during Season 5, except you can activate it whenever and wherever you need to. Once you grab this item, carry it in your soldier's backpack until it's needed. The moment you activate it, your soldier gets catapulted into the sky. You're then able to use the navigational controls to choose a landing spot.

One benefit to using a Rift-to-Go, as opposed to a Launch Pad, is that there's no setup. To use a Launch Pad, you often need to build a floor tile, and then place the Launch Pad on top of it. Then your soldier needs to step on the Launch Pad to be catapulted into the air. With a Rift-to-Go, when you select this item from your soldier's backpack and activate it, your soldier will be airborne in seconds. Your soldier can then glide through the air (not just go up and then down), so he or she will be able to travel a decent distance. The soldier's glider gets deployed to ensure a safe and precise landing at your desired location.

When it was first introduced, a Spiky Stadium was only available for a limited time within a Squads version of Playground mode. It's collected and then activated like a Port-a-Fort, but once it's used, a giant arena is instantly built. The walls of the arena are wallpapered with Traps and Bouncer Pads. This is the perfect place to host a practice battle between you and your Squad members. In the future, this item may get vaulted and then re-introduced with slight variations in other game play modes.

These two loot items were added near the very end of Season 5. Both can be used to quickly transport your soldier to another area, but each is used in a slightly different way. When a Shockwave Grenade gets detonated, it sends either your soldier, or nearby enemy soldiers, flying outward with incredible force. No damage is incurred when the soldier lands, however. As a weapon, for example, it can be used to force enemies out of a fortress they're hiding in.

When your soldier aims and shoots a Grappler, the plunger-like device juts forward and attaches to its target. Your soldier then quickly gets pulled to that target. It can be used to quickly reach the top of a building, to rush an enemy, or to swing like Spider-Man in-between structures or buildings, for example.

On an ongoing basis, as Epic Games releases game updates, new loot items are constantly being introduced, while other items get vaulted (meaning they're removed from the game but could be re-introduced at any time in the future).

It's important to become acquainted with each of the available loot items so you can determine which ones to grab and keep in your arsenal, and then know exactly how to best use them when the time is right.

To make the best use of the powerup loot items that can be used as weapons, tap your own creativity, and watch how other gamers use them. When working with any type of explosive loot item, make sure your soldier keeps a safe distance away and does not get caught in the explosion they've caused.

When tossing a Grenade at a structure or fortress, throw it through an open window or door, or down into a structure that contains no roof. Remember, if you toss a Grenade or aim a Grenade Launcher (shown here) at a solid wall or object, the Grenade will bounce back toward your soldier. The resulting explosion will wind up close to your soldier and have little or no impact on the actual target. Here, the Grenade Launcher is being aimed at a window in the fortress. If it goes through the window, it'll explode inside the fortress and cause serious damage to whoever is inside. But, if it bounces off of the wall, the fortress will receive minimal damage and the soldier(s) inside will remain safe.

Popular Loot Items That Can Be Used as Weapons

The following is information about some of the more popular loot items that can be used as weapons.

LOOT ITEM	DAMAGE	MAXIMUM NUMBER YOU CAN CARRY	STORAGE LOCATION
Boogie Bombs	Once detonated (by tossing it at an enemy), this bomb causes a soldier to dance uncontrollably for 5 seconds. During this time he or she is defenseless against other weapon or explosive attacks.	10	Requires one backpack inventory slot.
Bouncer Pads	If positioned correctly, these can be used to send an enemy into a bouncing loop, during which time, he or she will be defenseless against other types of attack. To use it as a weapon, you need to be creative.	Unknown	Stored with a soldier's resources, so it's accessed from Building mode, not Combat mode.
Clingers	Up to 100 HP damage can be caused if a soldier or object is caught in the explosion. Use this to defeat enemies or blow up objects or structures.	10	Requires one backpack inventory slot.

(Continued on next page)

Grenades	Up to 105 HP damage can be caused if a soldier or object is caught in the explosion. Use these to defeat enemies or blow up objects or structures.	10	Requires one backpack inventory slot.
Impulse Grenades	When thrown at enemies, this special grenade will catapult an enemy soldier away from the explosion's point of impact. This item does not damage structures or objects.	10	Requires one backpack inventory slot.
Remote Explosives	Damage to enemy soldiers varies, based on how close a target is to the explosion. If placed on a structure or object, it will blow it up. Use multiple Remote Explosives together to create a bigger bang. If you want to booby trap an ATK or Loot Llama, for example, this is the item to use.	10	Requires one backpack inventory slot.
Shockwave Grenades	When tossed, this type of grenade will send whoever is in its path flying backwards. This is more powerful than an Impulse Grenade but causes no actual damage when a soldier lands from their fall. This item can also be used to escape an area quickly.	6	Requires one backpack inventory slot.
Spiky Stadium	Available in Playground mode only. This item works like a Port-a-Fort but expands into a massive arena with walls that are covered with Traps and Bouncer Pads. This item is added and removed from the game periodically.	1	Requires one backpack slot.
Stink Bombs	Once tossed, a Stink Bomb generates a toxic cloud of yellow smoke that lasts for 9 seconds. For every half-second an enemy is caught in the smoke, they receive 5 HP damage. This weapon works best when deployed in a confined area (such as inside a structure).	4	Requires one backpack inventory slot.
Traps	A Trap can be placed on a wall, floor, or ceiling – within a structure built by a soldier or a pre-existing building, for example. If an enemy gets caught by a Trap, they'll perish.	No limit	Stored with a soldier's resources, so it's accessed from Building mode, not Combat mode.

Popular Powerup Loot Items

The following is information about some of the more popular loot items that can be used to replenish your soldier's Health and/or Shield meter.

LOOT ITEM	HOW LONG IT TAKES TO USE OR CONSUME	POWERUP BENEFIT	STORAGE LOCATION	MAXIMUM NUMBER YOU CAN CARRY
Apples	Almost Instantly	Increases your soldier's Health meter by 5 points per Apple consumed.	Apples must be consumed when and where they're found (which is usually under trees). They cannot be carried and used later.	None
Bandages	4 seconds	Increases your soldier's Health meter by 15 points.	Requires one backpack inventory slot.	15
Chug Jug	15 seconds	Replenishes your soldier's Health *and* Shield meter to 100.	Requires one backpack inventory slot.	1
Cozy Campfire	25 seconds	Boosts each soldier's Health by 2 points for every second he or she is standing near the flames for up to 25 seconds. If fully utilized, it boosts a soldier's Health meter by 50 points.	Stored with a soldier's resources, so it's accessed from Building mode, not Combat mode.	Unknown
Med Kits	10 seconds	Replenishes your soldier's Health meter back to 100.	Requires one backpack inventory slot.	3
Mushrooms	Almost instantly	Increases your soldier's Shield meter by 5 points (up to 100).	Mushrooms must be consumed when and where they're found. They cannot be carried and used later.	None
Shield Potion	5 seconds	Replenishes your soldier's Shield meter by 50 points (up to 100 maximum).	Requires one backpack inventory slot.	2

(Continued on next page)

| Slurp Juice | Approximately 2 seconds to consume and 37.5 seconds to achieve its full benefit. | A soldier's Health *and* Shield meter increases by one point (up to 75 points) for every half-second this drink is being consumed. | Requires one backpack inventory slot. | 1 |
| Small Shield Potion | 2 seconds | Replenishes your soldier's Shield meter by 25 points (up to 100). | Requires one backpack inventory slot. | 10 |

Loot Items that Can Be Used as Survival Tools

The following are additional loot items available during a match. These can be used as tools to help you survive longer or transport yourself around while on the island.

LOOT ITEM	HOW IT'S USED	BENEFITS & LIMITATIONS	DURATION OF USE
Bouncer Pad	In addition to being used as a weapon, it can be used to catapult your own soldier up into the air. He or she will land with zero damage.	A Bouncer Pad does not allow your soldier to reach the same altitude as a Launch Pad, but unlike a Launch Pad, it can be placed on a ramp tile, as well as any other flat surface.	Once placed, a Bouncer Pad can be used repeatedly, but it can't be relocated.
Bush Loot Item	Wear this item as camouflage and your soldier will look like a bush when he or she is standing still. Use this as a way to hide from enemies when outside.	While a Bush will hide you, it offers zero protection. If you get spotted, an enemy will attack you, and the Bush will immediately disappear.	Until it's destroyed, the Bush will provide camouflage. If you crouch down and remain still, you typically won't get spotted. If you walk around while wearing the Bush, you'll immediately attract attention.

Grappler	Shoot this item at a nearby target and as soon as it makes contact, your soldier will be catapulted forwards, toward the target area.	It's a quick way to reach higher-up (or lower-down) areas without sustaining injury. Use it to rush enemies or move to another location fast with no setup. You can also use this item repeatedly to swing from target to target, like Spider-Man.	Each time you add a Grappler to your arsenal, it offers 15 shots.
Launch Pads	Place a Launch Pad on a flat surface and then jump on it. Your soldier will be catapulted into the air. Use the directional controls to navigate as they fall (and then glide) back to land.	The same Launch Pad can be used many times by any soldier who jumps on it. Use it to quickly reach the top of a building, to escape a fortress that's under attack, or to help your soldier escape the storm.	Once you determine where and when it gets placed, a Launch Pad remains there until it's manually destroyed (by shooting at it or blowing it up).
Port-A-Forts	After collecting a Port-A-Fort, toss it at the desired building location, and the fort will be created instantly—without requiring any resources.	During the first few seconds as it's being built, a Port-A-Fort is somewhat vulnerable to attack. An enemy soldier can enter with you or follow you into the fort later. You definitely want to seal the entranceway.	A Port-A-Fort will offer protection until it's destroyed by enemy gunfire or an explosive weapon. Like any other type of structure, it too can be destroyed. However, because it's made from metal, it can withstand a lot of damage.
Port-A-Fortress	This item works like a Port-a-Fort, but the structure that's built is larger. It also has built-in Traps and Bouncer Pads on the outside walls.	Create this type of fort when you need quick protection during a battle. Use the built-in Bouncer Pads if you need to make a quick escape. This item is rarer than a Port-a-Fort, so if you find one, save it for when it'll be most useful, such as during the End Game.	A Port-A-Fortress will offer protection until it's destroyed by enemy gunfire or an explosive weapon. Like any other type of structure, it too can be destroyed. However, because it's made from metal, it can withstand a lot of damage.
Rift-to-Go	Use this item to quickly get catapulted into the air and be able to navigate to a desired (nearby) landing spot.	This item works like a Launch Pad or Bouncer Pad but requires no setup. It also catapults your soldier higher into the air.	Each Rift-to-Go item can only be used once. Use it to make a fast emergency escape or to relocate yourself.

The Island Is Continuously Evolving

Thanks to weekly or biweekly game updates (called "patches") from Epic Games, new points of interest that are not labeled on the map are frequently added, and existing points of interest sometimes get altered slightly. Beyond that, every three months or so, in conjunction with a new season of game play, entirely new points of interest are added to the island, and significant changes are typically made to the island's geography and the island map.

Each time something new is added, a News screen, like this one, appears when you launch *Fortnite: Battle Royale*. You can also discover what's new by visiting the official *Fortnite: Battle Royale* website at: www.epicgames.com/fortnite/en-US/news.

One way to get around quickly and be able to reach each point of interest on the island is to drive an ATK, which is why this unofficial guide offers a driving tour of the island. Keep in mind, the locations (points of interest) you read about within this guide (particularly in Section 3) may be updated or changed as Epic Games releases new game updates during Season 6 and beyond.

Even though points of interest change, how you should handle surviving and fighting when exploring various terrain types is explored in detail within this guide, so regardless of where you visit, by reading each section, you'll be better prepared for the challenges that await when you get there.

Keep in mind, within this unofficial guide, most of the screenshots were taken on a PS4 using the temporary Playground game play mode. As a result, some information displayed on the screen, such as the location of the storm, the timer, and the whereabouts of squad mates (if applicable) will be different than when playing other game play modes, like Solo, Duos, or Squads. Also, the location of information you see on the screen will vary, based on which gaming system you're using to play *Fortnite: Battle Royale*.

But before you focus on exploring the island, it's important to learn how to drive an ATK and discover the awesome capabilities of these vehicles. While you don't need a driver's license, having top-notch driving skills is a must. To learn more, simply turn the page and start reading the next section!

SECTION 2

LEARN TO DRIVE AN ALL TERRAIN KART— NO LICENSE REQUIRED

When you're ready to explore the island at a faster speed than ever before, simply locate an All Terrain Kart (ATK) once you land on the island, hop in, and put the pedal to the metal as you whiz around the island.

At the start of a match, if you're among the first soldiers to reach the racetrack area in the desert (located outside of Paradise Palms at map coordinates J6.5), or you land at Lazy Links (found at map coordinates F2.5), you'll likely discover an ATK in a garage or sitting outside. ATKs also become available at other random locations at the start of each match. For example, they often appear parked on the street in Tilted Towers and near the homes within Snobby Shores.

As you search homes located throughout the island, you will sometimes discover an ATK parked in the garage.

To take control of an ATK as the driver, walk up to the driver's side of the vehicle and press the Drive button on your controller (or keyboard/mouse).

Once you're in the driver's seat, displayed on the left side of the screen are the controller (keyboard/mouse) buttons used to drive the vehicle.

The main controls for driving an ATK include:

- **Switch Seat**—An ATK vehicle has two seats in the front, and space for two soldiers to stand in the back. How many soldiers you'll be able to transport will depend on which game play mode you've selected.
- **Forward**—Press the Forward button on the controller (mouse/keyboard) to drive forward. This is the gas pedal. As long as you keep this button pressed, the ATK will move in a forward direction until it hits a solid object that it can't smash through. Once you're traveling in a forward direction, use the directional controls on the controller to turn left or right, and to adjust your viewing direction and angle.
- **Brake / Reverse**—To stop the vehicle, simply remove your finger from the Forward button on the controller. If you need to make a sudden stop, release the Forward button and immediately

press the Brake button. To move the vehicle backward (in reverse), press just the Reverse button, and then use the directional controls to navigate. You'll quickly discover it's much easier to turn and steer while going forward.

Throughout many parts of the island, especially in and around Paradise Palms and the desert area of the island, along with the Lazy Links area, you'll discover paved roads like this one you can drive along. You will need to avoid broken-down cars and other obstacles in the road, however.

Powerslide—As you're driving, press the Powerslide button to make the rear tires spin extra fast. Once the sparks turn into flames, release the Powerslide button and the ATK will shoot forward at a fast speed. Powerslide is also used to make sharp turns while moving fast.

Exit—As the driver of an ATK, all you can do is steer the vehicle. You can't shoot or build at the same time. However, if you quickly stop and exit the ATK, you can immediately start shooting at enemies with whichever weapon your soldier is holding. You'll jump out of the vehicle and find yourself standing beside it with the selected weapon drawn and ready to fire. Make sure you hit the brake before leaping from the ATK, or the vehicle will keep traveling forward without you and eventually come to a stop.

What's truly awesome about driving an ATK is that you can go off-road and travel pretty much anywhere on the island, regardless of the terrain. For example, you can drive on dirt or grassy areas.

An ATK can travel up or down steep hills with no difficulty.

Normally, if your soldier is walking or running around the island, if he or she were to leap off a cliff, they'd be injured upon landing. The soldier's Health meter would take a huge hit. Shields don't protect against falls. However, when driving an ATK, you're able to drive right off the edge of a cliff and fall to the ground from almost any height, and not suffer any damage to your soldier.

When you come across a location on the island that's high up, but you don't see a path or road that'll get you to that location (such as the top of this stone bridge), one option is to build a ramp and then drive straight up (or down) it. If the vehicle accidently falls off the ramp, or the ramp gets destroyed, no worries. You'll likely land safely.

won't be injured, but the driver will need to exit the vehicle and then use the Flip command to get the ATK upright and ready to drive again.

Another way to take the ATK airborne is to drive directly into a Rift. The vehicle (with you in it) will be catapulted into the air, and you'll be able to navigate a bit as it falls back toward land. A passenger can also activate a Rift-to-Go while riding in an ATK, but this is not possible for the driver to do.

Is there water in your path? Perhaps you want to reach an object in the middle of a lake or take a shortcut across a lake. Well, an ATK can travel through water. Just like when a soldier decides to walk or run through water, this is a very slow process, but it is possible. A much better approach is to build a bridge over the water and then drive over it.

If you push an ATK to its limits, especially if you take it airborne, it might not always land on its four tires. As you can see, it's possible to flip an ATK over. In most cases, your soldier

A passenger can build while the ATK is in motion. If you're the driver and there are no passengers, you will need to exit the ATK in order to build a bridge or ramp, and then re-enter the vehicle to drive over what you've built.

To pick up speed, use the Powerslide feature and wait for the tires to appear as if they've caught on fire before releasing the Powerslide button, which causes the ATK to shoot forward.

Sure, you can take an ATK for a casual drive as you travel from one point of interest on the island to another, but your travels will be more fun when you go off-road and smash into smaller objects, like trees. Crashing into larger objects will cause damage to your vehicle and some of its HP will get depleted.

When playing in Duos, Squads, or a 50 v 50 mode, for example, two or more soldiers can drive within an ATK at once. As the vehicle is in motion, any or all of the passengers can use their weapons to shoot enemies or objects in any direction.

As you're driving or riding in an ATK, enemies can and will shoot at you as well. If bullets are flying at your soldier's ATK, the driver should speed up and take evasive maneuvers by driving in an unpredictable, zig-zag pattern. Passengers can shoot back but can be hit (and be injured or defeated) by an enemy's bullets. A driver can also be shot at and get injured or defeated by an enemy attack.

Each time the ATK hits an object, a small amount of its 400 HP will be depleted. It's best to avoid crashing head-on into objects or larger size structures. When the vehicle's HP hits zero, it'll be destroyed and disappear. Likewise, if you leave the vehicle for more than a few minutes, it'll likely disappear or be taken over by another soldier.

An ATK has 400 HP and can withstand direct hits from a few bullets but is no match for a weapon that continuously fires powerful bullets from close range, or from any type of explosive weapon, such as Grenades, Clingers, or the rockets from a Rocket Launcher, Guided Missile Launcher, or Grenade Launcher. Here, the soldier is shooting an empty ATK, and the bullets are slowly reducing the vehicle's HP. Its HP meter is shown here in the center of the screen.

One hit with an explosive weapon (in this case a Clinger), and the ATK gets instantly destroyed. In this situation, if the vehicle had a driver or passengers, they'd either be injured or defeated, depending on the level of their Health and Shield meters, and how much of the explosion's impact they received.

During a match, you'll hear the roar of an ATK's engine from a distance. Once you spot it, start shooting using any type of weapon. Try using a rifle with a scope to snipe at the driver or passengers and hit 'em with a headshot. This will prove to be a challenge, since they'll be a fast-moving target. Another option is to toss Grenades or Clingers at the ATK, but you'll need to be close to the vehicle to hit it. Especially if a driver is alone in the vehicle, he or she is vulnerable while driving, since it's not possible to drive and shoot at the same time.

If you need to stop abruptly and escape from the vehicle due to an incoming attack that you can't defend against, jump onto the back of the ATK and it serves as a Bounce Pad. Your soldier will catapult into the air. While airborne, use the directional controls to put some distance between your soldier and the vehicle.

Becoming a skilled driver of an ATK takes practice, especially if you want to use the Powerslide feature to make high-speed turns, or to launch the vehicle forward at a high speed. If Playground mode is available, use it to practice your driving skills and experiment while driving to learn firsthand what an ATK can withstand, and what will cause it to be destroyed and disappear.

A few weeks after ATKs were introduced, Epic Games added the ability to honk the vehicle's horn while driving. Obviously when you do this, it makes noise, which will alert enemies of your location. However, some gamers use the horn as a signal for their squad mates when playing a Duos or Squads match. For example, three quick honks could mean load back into the vehicle to move out.

Another option is to visit the racetrack area outside of Paradise Palms, and practice racing around the track. It contains sharp turns to navigate around, so you can practice using the Powerslide feature. If you approach the starting line of the racetrack, the countdown will be displayed, and when the green light appears, start driving. You'll be timed as you race around the track. This is one way to put your driving skills to the test.

During matches, an ATK can be used to help you outrun the storm, or to travel between various points of interest much faster than you could otherwise travel by walking or running, for example.

Now that you know how to get around while driving an ATK, let's take a tour of the island. Within the next section, the island's most popular locations (points of interest) are listed in alphabetical order. With each location description, you'll discover a bunch of useful tips and strategies that'll help you stay alive longer and defeat your enemies while visiting that location.

SECTION 3

AN "A TO Z" ISLAND TOUR AND SURVIVAL GUIDE

Thanks to Playground mode, Solo mode, and some of *Fortnite: Battle Royale*'s other gameplay modes, you're able to take a leisurely driving tour of the island by first picking up an All Terrain Kart at the racetrack located outside of Paradise Palms (at map coordinates J7), for example.

How to Read the Island Map

The full island map is divided into quadrants (boxes). Displayed along the top margin of the map (from left to right) are the letters "A" through "J." Along the left margin of the map, from top to bottom, are the numbers "1" through "10." Using these letters and numbers, you can easily identify any location or quadrant on the map.

For example, quadrant F2.5 on the map corresponds with Lazy Links, while coordinates H6 corresponds with Retail Row. Lucky Landing can be found between coordinates F10 and G10. The Viking village (which contains a ship) can be found on an unlabeled mountain, near map coordinates B5.5.

An "A to Z" Guide to Points of Interest

Throughout this section, we'll explore each of the labeled points of interest on the island map, plus point out a few other "must see" locations that are not labeled. Each location is featured here in alphabetical order for easy reference.

C

Cargo Storage Facilities

Located in several places on the island, including at map coordinates H4.5, are cargo container storage facilities, like this one. It's typically safer to stay as high up as possible in areas like this. This way, you can shoot downward at enemies who are on ground level, without getting lost in the maze-like area that the containers create.

On ground level, you can hide in containers, and sometimes find chests, weapons, ammo, or loot items lying on the ground inside them. Using Remote Explosives, for example, you can boobytrap a container, or hide around a corner and wait for an enemy to come around a turn before launching a surprise attack. Here, the soldier purposely dropped Bandages in the container where he also activated Remote Explosives. He can now hide and wait for an enemy to enter before detonating the Remote Explosives. You can tell the Remote Explosives are active by the blue flashing light each of them displays once they've been placed.

If you stay at ground level, you're likely to be shot at from enemy soldiers who have a height advantage. You're better off staying on top of the cargo containers or in the surrounding buildings.

Surrounding this structure are several buildings. If you either land on or get to the roof of this one, you'll see the golden glare of a chest coming through the roof.

Around the outside of this container storage facility you'll discover wooden pallets. Using your pickaxe, smash these pallets to harvest a lot of wood.

As you're exploring any area of the island, you'll likely discover weapons and ammo lying on the ground, out in the open. Some will be located on top of containers, not just inside them.

Learn How to Determine a Weapon's Strength

While every weapon has the ability to cause damage and potentially defeat your adversaries, each is rated based on several criteria, including its rarity. Weapons are color-coded with a hue around them to showcase their rarity.

Instead of attempting to reach this chest on ground level, this soldier is waiting patiently for an enemy to approach it. He'll then shoot at the enemy from above. Using a sniper rifle (with a scope) would be ideal for this task, but any mid-to-long-range gun will do the trick.

Weapons with a **gray** hue are "Common." Weapon with a **green** hue are "Uncommon." Weapons with a **blue** hue (shown here) are "Rare."

Weapons with a **purple** hue are "Epic." "Legendary" weapons, with an **orange** hue (shown here), are hard to find, extra powerful, and very rare. If you're able to obtain one, grab it! Guided Missiles are one of the newer explosive projectile weapons added to *Fortnite: Battle Royale*. Other projectile weapons, which are powerful long-range weapons that cause explosions, include Grenade Launchers and Rocket Launchers. All three are great for destroying structures (and defeating whoever is inside them).

One easy way to reach the top of the crate in order to grab the Guided Missile Launcher that's up there is to jump on the back of the ATK and use its built-in Bouncer Pad. If you can find one, a Grappler loot item is also very useful for quickly reaching high places.

It is possible to collect several of the same weapon, but each could have a different rarity. So, if you collect two of the same weapon and one is rare, but the second is legendary, definitely keep the legendary weapon and trade the other for something else when you find a replacement.

If you're really interested in how a weapon is rated, evaluate its DPR (Damage Per Second) rating, overall Damage Rating, Fire Rate, MAG (Magazine) Capacity, and Reload Time. This is information that Epic Games tweaks often. Select a weapon when viewing your Backpack Inventory screen to see details about it.

There are also plenty of websites, including: IGN. com (www.ign.com/wikis/fortnite/Weapons), Gameskinny.com (www.gameskinny.com/9mt22 /complete-fortnite-battle-royale-weapons-stats-list), and RankedBoost.com (https:// rankedboost.com/fortnite/best-weapons-tier-list), that provide the current stats for each weapon offered in *Fortnite: Battle Royale*, based on the latest tweaks made to the game. Just make sure when you look at this information online, it refers to the most recently released version of *Fortnite: Battle Royale*.

D

Dusty Divot

Located between map coordinates F5.5 and G5.5, at the start of Season 5, Dusty Divot got a facelift. Instead of being an active research facility, it's now been abandoned. Within the small buildings and structures that remain, you'll likely discover chests, weapons, ammo, loot items, and resource icons—that is, if you're the first soldier to reach the area and grab what's there.

On the outskirts of Dusty Divot, you'll discover two large warehouse structures. Both contain useful weapons, ammo, loot items, and resource icons that are worth grabbing.

One wall to this warehouse is missing. A chest is almost always on the ledge. However, if you try to open the chest, all of its contents will fall to the ground below.

To keep the chest's contents from falling over the cliff, before opening it, build one wooden floor tile at the ledge.

When you're done visiting the two warehouses, travel down the hill and enter into what was once the Dusty Divot research facility. While

avoiding enemies, or in between firefights with them, search all of the remaining structures and the rooms within them.

On the top of nearby flatbed trucks, you'll often find weapons, ammo, or other items you might want to grab in order to build up or improve your arsenal.

Several of these strong doors remain intact and closed. If you notice one has been opened, this means an enemy soldier has already been here and could still be hiding behind the door. Each time you need to pass through a closed door, have your weapon drawn and proceed with caution.

When you discover a chest, make sure no enemies are nearby, and then open it to see what goodies are inside.

As always, if you get up to a higher level than your enemies, you'll be able to shoot at them as they pass below. Another option, if you see an enemy go into a structure, is to use an explosive weapon to destroy the entire structure, along with whoever is inside.

E

End Game

Every match you experience when playing *Fortnite: Battle Royale* ends with an End Game (also called the Final Circle).

The End Game begins once the storm has spread over much of the island and has left only a small area inhabitable. All of the soldiers who are still alive are forced into this small area and must fight for their survival, or they'll perish and be eliminated from the match.

During the End Game, you may want to build a fortress and then focus on using long-range weapons, such as a Sniper Rifle, Grenade Launcher, Rocket Launcher, or Guided Missile Launcher to attack your enemies from a distance. The Sniper Rifle allows you to shoot at enemies (and aim for a head shot), while the other projectile weapons cause explosions and will destroy fortresses, and likely injure or defeat everyone caught in the explosion.

Each Solo, Duos, or Squads match lasts about 15 minutes and concludes when one soldier (or squad) has defeated everyone else. The winner achieves #1 Victory Royale. Everyone else perishes and is eliminated from the match.

Inside the stable, you'll discover individual stalls. Within some of them, you'll often find weapons, ammo, and/or loot items out in the open.

F

Fatal Fields

In the loft area of the stables, you'll often discover a chest, but you'll need to build a ramp in order to reach it. Some chests always appear in the same place, match after match, so it's important to remember exactly where you find them. Sometimes, however, chests are placed randomly at the start of each match.

Fatal Fields (located between map coordinates F8 and G8) is one of the farming areas on the island. All are very similar in terms of the types of structures you'll encounter. In addition to wilted corn fields, you'll discover a handful of barns, farmhouses, silos, stables, and other structures, all spread out, with open area between them.

If you hear an enemy approaching, consider hiding within one of the stables. Close the door behind you, crouch down, wait for the soldier to approach . . . and then shoot! You'll always have more accurate aim if you crouch down and press the Aim button before pulling the trigger. Landing a headshot will almost always defeat an opponent with a single bullet. Otherwise, depending on the weapon you're using and how far you are from your target, it might take several body shots to defeat the enemy you're shooting at.

You'll almost always discover a chest somewhere on the top floor of the farm house.

If you hear enemies in the area, you have the option to hide behind haystacks. While this will likely keep you from being seen (if you remain quiet), keep in mind that haystacks offer zero protection if an enemy starts shooting. With one bullet hit, the haystack will disappear, and you'll be visible and out in the open.

This large barn has several levels. While you may discover useful things to collect that are lying out in the open on the ground, be sure to check behind hay stacks.

Anytime you come across silos, smash them. You'll often discover a chest within at least one of them. While you can shoot the silo, you're better off using your soldier's pickaxe to smash it. This way you can collect some metal as well.

The farmhouse is just like many of the homes on the island, but this one has lots of rooms.

Check inside the bathroom. You'll see a break in the wall that leads to a secret room. Inside there's a chest.

Like many houses on the island, you'll also discover a chest in the attic of the farmhouse. In this case, you might need to smash through a few wooden beams or a wall to reach it. If you don't see the chest right away, listen for the sound it makes.

Use your soldier's pickaxe to smash any vehicle, including tractors in any farm area, to harvest a bunch of metal. Smashing vehicles makes noise. The commotion might attract enemies and reveal your location. Keep in mind, if you smash a car, in addition to the sound caused by hitting the metal with a pickaxe, the car's security alarm will also go off, which generates even more noise.

Anytime you build a structure or fortress and it receives damage from an incoming attack, your soldier has the ability to repair the damage. To do this, face the damaged tile and press the Repair button on your controller or keyboard.

While a repair is underway, you will see "+" icons. The tile itself will also become less translucent and eventually become solid again as its HP gets replenished. In some cases, it makes sense to repair a structure or fortress and use up resources. In other situations, it'll make more sense to abandon the structure and rebuild somewhere that's safer. It all depends on how strong the incoming attack is and whether or not you have a chance to defeat the enemy.

Flush Factory

The next stop on our driving tour of the island is Flush Factory. It's located at map coordinates D9.5. There's not much here, aside from a large toilet factory.

If you enter through the front door of the factory, you'll come across this office and toilet showroom. Chances are, if you're the first one to visit here during a match, you'll find a few useful items lying on the ground waiting to be picked up. Proceed through the door in the back of the office to enter into the main factory area.

The factory area has two main levels. When you know enemies are nearby, stick to the higher levels. The most useful weapons, loot items, and ammo can typically be found in the small rooms and areas that surround the factory floor.

On the top of this room you'll often (but not always) discover a chest. To reach it, proceed to the second level and then build a bridge.

An additional chest can often be found out in the open, on the factory's second level. If you happen to find a Port-A-Fort, this is a particularly rare but very useful loot item. You can carry it within your backpack until it's needed. It'll take up one slot in your soldier's backpack.

At the end of Season 5, a new and more powerful type of Port-A-Fort, called a Port-A-Fortress, was added to the game, so be on the lookout for it. It's a rare loot item.

How to Utilize a Port-A-Fort

When you need to very quickly create a metal fortress, use a Port-A-Fort. Find an open area and toss the Port-A-Fort item from your soldier's backpack. Within a second or two, a tall, metal fort will be constructed. This does not require any resources.

Open the door to the fortress and step inside. Jump on the tires to quickly leap to the top of the fortress. Keep in mind, an enemy soldier can follow you inside, so watch your back. As a Port-A-Fort is actually being constructed, for a few seconds, it is vulnerable to an enemy's attack or forced entry into it, so be prepared for this.

As soon as you reach the top of the fort, to keep an enemy from following you inside, quickly build a metal floor tile in the center. Then, on top of that metal floor tile, build a pyramid tile. Doing this will definitely slow an enemy down if they try to invade your fortress.

Select a long-range weapon, such as a Guided Missile Launcher, Rocket Launcher, or Grenade Launcher, peek over the top of the fortress, and start shooting at enemies or their fortresses.

If you need to replenish your health while hiding out in a Port-A-Fort, instead of building the pyramid tile in the center, just build a metal floor tile. On top of that, place a Cozy Campfire. Once it's activated, over the next 25 seconds, any soldiers that stand close to the flame will have their Health meter replenished by 2 points per second.

A Health meter maxes out at 100 HP points, so a Cozy Campfire can replenish up to half of it. Place two Cozy Campfires on top of each other to double the Health healing capabilities of this loot item.

G

Greasy Grove

Located near map coordinates C7, this is a small suburban area that contains a handful of single-family houses, fast-food restaurants, a gas station, and a shop. If you're looking to build up your arsenal, it's the houses you want to search.

Go inside this fast-food restaurant to see if any weapons, ammo, or loot items are lying on the ground, waiting to be grabbed. If you see or hear an enemy in the area, crouch down behind the counter and ambush them as they approach.

Inside the two-level store, you'll discover at least one chest, along with weapons, ammo, loot items, and resource icons lying on the ground. The inside balcony on the second floor offers a great vantage point from which you can shoot at enemy soldiers as they enter the building.

Once inside a house, the easiest way to reach the attic is to go to the top floor, and then build a ramp that leads to the ceiling. Climb the ramp and use your soldier's pickaxe to smash through the ceiling to gain entrance to the attic. Look within the attic for a chest. If the attic is divided up into separate sections, you may need to smash through some walls to reach the chest. Listen carefully for the sound of a chest if you can't immediately see one.

While inside any house, use your soldier's pick-axe to smash furniture, appliances, walls, and other objects in order to harvest resources. Depending on what the object you're smashing is made from, this will determine the type of resource you gather. Smashing objects within a house makes noise. Keep an eye out for enemies who may try to sneak up on you, because you might not hear their footsteps if there's too much noise in the area.

There are several houses located within Greasy Grove. Virtually all houses you discover on the island have at least two levels. Most also have an attic and/or basement, and some have a garage. It's within these areas that you're most apt to find a chest.

As you approach a house, if you think one or more enemies may already be inside, instead of walking through the front door and running the risk of being attacked, peek through the windows to see if you spot anyone. You can always shoot at enemies from outside the house through a window. Another option is to toss Grenades or Clingers through a window, or to shoot and attempt to destroy portions of the house (with your enemies inside) using a Rocket Launcher, Grenade Launcher, or Guided Missile Launcher.

As you walk around the outside of a house, if you spot a dog house, check inside. You may discover a chest. Watch for its glow and listen for its sound as you approach. Smash the dog house with your pickaxe to reveal the chest, and then open it.

From outside the house, if you notice the front or back door is already open, this means someone else has already entered the structure and may still be inside. In this case, you can enter with your gun drawn and be ready to fight, or you can take cover outside the house, wait for the enemy to exit, and then attack them. If you're able to defeat the enemy as they're leaving the house, you'll be able to collect all of the weapons, ammo, and resources he or she was carrying, including everything that soldier discovered while exploring the house.

The fast-food restaurant is the main building in Greasy Grove. It looks like a two-story building, but there's also a full basement, plus a roof you can climb up to.

Don't forget to check inside the bathrooms to see what you can find lying on the ground.

Head down to the basement. You'll likely find a chest, plus several additional items on the ground. This is a great place to plan an ambush for enemies if you know they're nearby.

Place a Trap on a wall down the hall a bit from the staircase (so it can't easily be seen), and then stand on the opposite corner of the basement with your gun aimed near the entrance to the room. If the Trap doesn't defeat the enemy that comes downstairs after you, your bullets certainly will.

Scattered randomly throughout the island, and sometimes found within Greasy Grove, are Vending Machines. Each Vending Machine offers a different selection of weapons or loot items you can purchase using wood, stone, or metal as money. Buying one or more powerful weapons is a great way to increase your arsenal, especially before an End Game. However, make sure you don't spend resources you may need to build fortresses or structures during the End Game. Here, a Hunting Rifle was purchased from the Vending Machine.

When you walk up to a Vending Machine, one at a time you'll see the items displayed that are available. Press the appropriate button on the controller (or keyboard mouse) to exchange resources for the desired item. The item you select will appear at your feet. If it's a weapon, it'll include ammo.

Instead of making a purchase from a Vending Machine, another strategy is to hide out near a Vending Machine. Wait for an enemy to buy something, and then attack them. If you defeat that enemy, you'll collect everything they were carrying, as well as whatever they just purchased. To protect yourself from this happening to you, consider building walls around yourself and the Vending Machine before you make a purchase.

H

Haunted Hills

Located at map coordinates B2.5, this is one of the creepier areas of the island. It's a relatively small point of interest that contains two churches, a few stone crypts, and a bunch of tombstones. Smashing the tombstones and stone structures allows you to harvest a lot of stone while you're here.

The large church with the tower typically contains multiple chests. Some are out in the open and easy to spot. Others are behind walls that you'll need to smash through in order to reach them.

Once inside the church that contains a tower, look for chests that are easy to spot. Next, smash through the floor. You'll discover a basement below that often contains an additional chest.

If you suspect there are enemy soldiers within Haunted Hills at the same time as you're there, climb to the top of the church's tower and use it as a lookout. As you spot enemies below, shoot at them. As always, this works best if you're using a sniper rifle with a scope, but any mid-to long-range weapon will do the trick.

While you're visiting Haunted Hills, be sure to peek inside the smaller stone crypts. You'll often discover weapons, ammo, and/or loot

items lying on the ground, out in the open. These small stone structures also make good hiding places. You can crouch down inside with a weapon drawn, and then shoot at enemies that try to enter. Remember, if you smash anything made of stone using your soldier's pickaxe, including the buildings, you can harvest stone. If you're going to spend time in Haunted Hills, don't leave without increasing your stash of stone.

J

Junk Junction

Throughout the island, there are several junk yards. Junk Junction, which is found at map coordinates C1.5, contains tall piles of junk vehicles. From a strategy standpoint, treat this area just as you would one of the Cargo Container Storage Facilities.

If you stay at ground level, you'll discover that the car piles create a maze-like area. You won't be able to see around turns, so it's easy for enemies to hide and launch surprise attacks, either from ground level or above.

Your best bet in this area is to stick to the higher-up areas. Climb to the top of the car piles (or build ramps to get there), and then be ready to shoot at enemies below you.

While you'll likely find at least one or two chests, along with weapons, ammo, and loot items lying out in the open on ground level,

it's within the buildings that surround the junk yard area where you're most apt to find chests and other useful items that'll help you build your arsenal.

To quickly reach the top of a building, you have three options. Go inside and climb up the stairs, build a ramp on the outside of the building that goes from ground level to the roof, or look for a pile of tires near the side of a building and jump on the tires.

With so much metal all around you, be sure to use the pickaxe to smash vehicles to harvest metal . . . a lot of metal.

The Ups and Downs of Building Ramps on the Island

One potential problem with building a tall ramp and standing on top of it is that an enemy can shoot at and destroy just one tile near the bottom or middle of the ramp, and the whole thing will come crashing down. (Your soldier will fall, and potentially perish, if this happens). If the ramp is made from metal, like this one, it can withstand a more intense attack, but eventually the ramp will collapse, especially after two or three hits from a Grenade Launcher, Rocket Launcher, or Guided Missile Launcher.

Knowing you want to be as high up as possible while in Junk Junction (or almost any area of the island for that matter), you always have the option of building a tall ramp.

At the top of the tall ramp, add a wall tile on either side to prevent someone from shooting directly at you from the side.

From the top of the tall ramp, use a long-range projectile weapon, a sniper rifle (with a scope), or any mid-to-long-range weapon to shoot at enemies below you.

Another option that works pretty much anywhere on the island is to build a double ramp. This requires more resources, but as you're climbing or standing on the ramps, you can leap back and forth between the two of them, and an enemy soldier below you won't be able to see your location. Plus, if one ramp is about to collapse, you can jump to the other and often buy yourself a few extra seconds before both ramps collapse.

As you're building a ramp to get up higher than your enemies, if you suspect that one or more of your adversaries is already higher up than you, and could shoot at you from above, build an Over-Under Ramp. At the same time you build a ramp below your feet to walk on, you'll build a ramp above your head to offer protection from attacks from above. This too takes up extra resources, but it's often worth it if you need the extra protection.

When you need to reach the top of a mountain, build a ramp along the side of it. This makes the ramp a lot stronger.

Normally, if one tile of a regular ramp gets destroyed, the whole ramp comes crashing down. When you build along the side of a mountain, individual ramp tiles can be destroyed, but the ramp will remain standing and functional (but with a gap, like the one shown on the right).

Consider building fancy ramps, like these, which can withstand more intense attacks and keep your soldier safer. These too require extra resources to build.

There's More to See Near Junk Junction

If you need to make a quick getaway from Junk Junction (or any other part of the island), consider building a tall ramp with a platform on top of it (using one floor tile). Next, place a Launch Pad on the platform tile.

Jump on the Launch Pad, and your soldier will be catapulted into the air. While soaring in the air, navigate to where you want your soldier to land. This can be a pretty good distance away from your original location.

If you're leaving Junk Junction by jumping on a Launch Pad, one nearby point of interest where you can land is a movie set. It's not labeled on the map. It can be found at map coordinates C1.5. You can also travel to this area by quickly driving an ATK, walking, or running to this location from Junk Junction, for example.

The movie set area is small. Inside the sound stage (where a movie is being filmed) there are two levels. Search the area, and you'll likely find one or two chests.

One chest can often be found on these shelves.

You'll need to build a ramp from the ground to reach the chest on the shelves.

Also located just outside of Junk Junction, up on a hill, is this massive llama-shaped tower that's made of metal. Go into the tower, and you'll discover chests and other useful items inside.

From the top of the llama-shaped tower, you'll get a bird's eye view of Junk Junction. If you have a projectile weapon, shoot at enemies you see off in the distance, or just spend time here collecting the weapons, ammo, and loot items you discover. When you're done, smash some or all of the tower to harvest a ton of metal.

Lazy Links

Lazy Links was added to the island as a new point of interest at the start of Season 5. This is a luxury golf course. Here, you'll discover a handful of buildings, all of which contain useful items and weapons to collect. It's also one of the places on the island where you're virtually guaranteed to find All Terrain Karts, assuming you're one of the first soldiers to reach this area.

In addition to finding ATKs outside on the roads, paths, and golf course, be sure to check within this garage area if you're looking to take a drive.

Outside of the main clubhouse there's a parking lot. There's typically not too much to discover here, but you can smash the parked cars to harvest some metal.

This is the back view of the main clubhouse at the golf course. Go inside and explore the different rooms and areas. Keep in mind, this is a very popular point of interest, so you'll likely encounter enemy soldiers lurking all around.

There are several small structures located around the golf course. The ones with a garage might contain an ATK. However, when you smash the garage door, you might discover a tractor instead.

Smash the tractor to collect metal and see what goodies may be behind it.

Throughout the island, including within the structures you explore within Lazy Links, check the shelves for Ammo Boxes. These green boxes do not glow, nor do they make a sound like chests. When you open an Ammo Box, inside will be a collection of ammo you can grab and then use with the various weapons in your arsenal.

Behind the main clubhouse is a swimming pool. Surrounding the pool are several covered bungalows and sun chairs. There's also often a Vending Machine in this area.

In the bungalows, check behind the counter and you'll often find a chest.

Be sure to smash this wall near the pool.

You'll almost always discover a hidden chest behind it. If you're not sure which wall to smash, listen for the sound of the chest. By smashing the walls, you'll also harvest some resources.

Within the gazebo that's near the lake, you'll often discover a chest. This area is out in the open, so watch out for snipers and enemies that might try shooting at you if you get spotted.

The sand traps on the golf course often have weapons, ammo, and/or loot items lying out in the open waiting to be grabbed. However, when you're exploring the golf course, you'll be out in the open and vulnerable to attack. If you're on foot, be ready to build walls around your soldier if someone starts shooting at you. If you're driving an ATK, take evasive action if you see or hear bullets or projectile weapons from enemies coming your way.

What fun is visiting a golf course if you can't play a round of golf, either alone or with your squad mates? Playing golf offers zero tactical advantage, but it's fun.

Before the match, add the golf ball as an emote to the Emotes menu. This is done from the Locker. Then, while you're on the golf course, access the Emotes menu and select the golf ball.

When you play golf, your soldier's pickaxe serves as his or her golf club. Try to line up your shot with one of the golf course's holes (which are marked by a flag), and see if you can hit a hole in one.

Lonely Lodge

Lonely Lodge, which is centered between map coordinates I5 and J5, is a camping ground. Here, you'll come across a main lodge, a bunch of small wooden cabins, and some RVs. You'll also see a bunch of trees and rock formations scattered throughout the area. Trees can be harvested for wood, while the rock formations can be harvested for stone using your soldier's pickaxe.

Go inside the large lodge and trek up to the second floor. You'll likely see this chest in a loft area.

Build one wooden floor tile that you can stand on (to fill in the gap) to reach the chest.

Assuming it's safe and there are no enemies nearby, approach the chest and open it to reveal the treasures that await inside.

Using your pickaxe, smash any RVs and vehicles you encounter in this area to harvest and collect metal. Before demolishing an RV, check its roof to make sure there are no items or weapons to collect.

Throughout Lonely Lodge are a handful of small wooden cabins. Inside you typically will not find chests, but there are often weapons, ammo, or loot items on the ground, out in the open.

If you go inside one of these small cabins, close the door behind you. Crouch down and point your weapon at the door as you wait for an enemy to enter behind you. As soon as the door opens, start shooting.

When you approach a cabin, if the front door is already open and you hear someone is inside, select a projectile weapon (in this case a Guided Missile Launcher was used), and shoot through the open door.

One round from a Guided Missile, Rocket Launcher, or Grenade Launcher is enough to destroy the entire cabin and blow up anyone who's inside.

From the top of the tower, you can see in all directions. Look out to the southeast and you'll get a great view of the Mega Mansion. See the listing for Mega Mansion in this guide to learn more about it.

As you leave the main area of Lonely Lodge, head toward this large wooden tower. If you're the first soldier to reach it during a match, you'll find several chests.

Use the stairs to climb to the top of the tower. Along the way, you'll likely find weapons, ammo, and loot items on the steps.

In the small cabin located at the top of the tower, you'll often find a chest on the shelf, along with at least one Ammo Box.

From the top of the tower, look to the southwest and you'll see an RV park. When you visit here, you'll be able to collect a bunch of weapons, ammo, and loot items, plus harvest a lot of metal by smashing the RVs with your pickaxe. If you look at the top-center of the screen, you'll see a moving compass that always shows you which direction you're facing.

Get to Know Your Ammo

Anytime you come across ammo, whether it's lying out in the open, within a chest, it comes from a Loot Llama or Supply Drop, or you pick it up after eliminating an enemy from the match, be sure to grab it!

There are five types of ammo available to collect. Each works with different categories of weapons. Rockets are the ammo used by Rocket Launchers, Grenade Launchers, and Guided Missile Launchers, which can be used anytime during a match. They're particularly useful during the End Game, so the more rounds of Rockets ammo you collect throughout the match, the more chances you'll have to make structures explode or eliminate enemies from a distance. Rocket ammo tends to be scarce, so it's important to stockpile it whenever you can.

In addition to being able to view your soldier's inventory and arsenal on the main game screen, the Backpack Inventory screen allows you to see additional information and learn more about a particular weapon or ammo type. From this screen, you're also able to re-organize which backpack slot a particular weapon or item is in. This is useful because it allows you to make your favorite, or most frequently used, weapons more easily accessible.

Remember, without ammunition, a weapon is useless. When you run out of ammo, a message stating, "Not Enough Ammo" and/or "Out of Ammo!" appears on the screen, plus your soldier will shake his or her head when you try to shoot.

The different types of ammunition include:

- **Heavy Bullets**—These bullets are used in sniper rifles and other high-caliber weapons that are designed for long-range shooting.
- **Light Bullets**—These bullets are used in pistols, SMGs, and most handheld guns. This type of ammo causes more damage when used at close range. To inflict the most damage, aim for a headshot or hit your target multiple times.
- **Medium Bullets**—These bullets are used in assault rifles and similar weapons. This type of ammo is ideal for mid-range shooting, although the closer you are, the more damage each bullet will inflict.
- **Rockets**—This is long-range explosive ammunition that's used with Rocket Launchers, Guided Missile Launchers, and Grenade Launchers. Even if you don't yet have one of these weapons in your personal arsenal, collect this ammo whenever you can and stockpile it. You can always share it with your partner or squad mates. Having a Rocket Launcher, Guided Missile Launcher, or Grenade Launcher will be extremely useful during the End Game.
- **Shells**—This type of ammo is used in shotguns. This ammo will inflict the most damage at close range, but shotguns can be used when you're at any distance from your target. The farther you are away, the less damage each direct hit will inflict.

Without having the appropriate ammunition, whatever weapons you're carrying will be useless. Throughout each match, there are several ways to find and collect ammo.

Loot Lake

Located around map coordinates E4 is the largest lake on the island. In the middle of the lake are two islands, one of which contains a house. Surrounding the lake are a handful of large and small structures.

You'll discover this massive wooden tower on the lake's edge. Climb to the top, and you'll likely find at least one chest along with other useful items.

From the top of the tower, you'll get a great view of the Loot Lake region. If you have a projectile weapon or sniper rifle, shoot at enemies below you, who are traveling across the lake, or those that are off in the distance.

This small structure with a dock that's located on the edge of a lake often (but not always) has a Vending Machine outside. Inside you'll sometimes find a chest, or at least one or two other useful weapons or loot items.

If you have an ATK, you can easily drive around the lake quickly. However, if you choose to cross the lake, you'll definitely want to build a ramp. This will require a bunch of resources. Using a ramp, you can easily reach either island located in the middle of the lake or reach the rowboat that often contains a chest that's parked in the lake.

When you're crossing the lake, either by walking through the water or by crossing a bridge that you've built, you'll be out in the open and vulnerable to attack. Be ready to build a quick structure to protect you from incoming bullets. This structure was created by building one ramp tile, and then placing two levels of wall tires around three sides of it. For better protection, this structure should be made from stone or metal.

A basic structure you can build just about anywhere when you need quick shielding is a wall tile with a ramp tile right behind it. Have your soldier crouch down behind the ramp for maximum shielding from an incoming attack. This structure is made from stone. Your enemy will need to destroy two layers of tiles before being able to harm your soldier with their bullets or projectile weapons.

If you build a Port-A-Fort in the middle of the lake, you'll be able to look out the top in any direction and shoot at your enemies who are below you or off in the distance. Any long-range weapon will work well in this situation.

Located along the edge of Loot Lake, near the wooden tower, is this modern-looking house. Explore it just as you would any house. You're apt to discover useful items within several of its rooms.

In the middle of the lake are two islands. The larger island has a house on it. This is a rather large house. If you're the first one to reach it during a match, you're virtually guaranteed to find an awesome selection of weapons, ammo, and loot items.

From the top floor of the house, point a mid-to long-range weapon out the window and get a clear line-of-sight to enemies located pretty far away.

As you drive around Loot Lake (or cross it), you'll encounter these two warehouses. Both contain chests, as well as weapons, ammo, and loot items. From the roof of either building, you will get a great view of the entire lake. From this vantage point, shoot at enemies as they cross the lake, or while they are visiting one of the islands in the middle of the lake, for example.

If your soldier is standing on the roof of a tall building, such as one of the warehouses along the edge of Loot Lake, one safe way to get back to the ground level quickly is to use a Bouncer Pad.

Place a Bouncer Pad on the roof or on a platform that juts out from the roof (shown here). Have your soldier step on the Bouncer Pad to go airborne. As he's landing, use the directional controls to choose a landing spot on ground level.

When using a Bouncer Pad, a soldier will always land safely (with no damage), no matter how high up he or she falls from.

Lucky Landing

You'll find this Asian-themed area at around map coordinates F10. Here you'll come across a variety of different types of buildings and structures. On the outskirts of the area is this large Asian temple. Inside you'll discover multiple chests, so it's worth exploring all its levels.

In the center of Lucky Landing is a giant pink tree that juts out from the center of a building.

Go into the structure and use your soldier's pickaxe to smash the large tree.

Once the tree is destroyed, you'll often (but not always) discover a chest.

There's one tall building in this area. Be sure to search all of the rooms found on each level, as you work your way to the top floor. Here you'll discover an office with a large window that overlooks most of Lucky Landing.

Using a Sniper Rifle (with a scope) or any mid-to long-range weapon, shoot at enemies you spot lurking around at ground level. As always, having a height advantage will be beneficial during a firefight.

When you visit the restaurants and shops here in Lucky Landing, be sure to check behind the counters. You'll often discover weapons, ammo, and/or loot items out in the open, or a chest might be there waiting for you to open it.

Behind this counter, the soldier spotted a Chug Jug. When consumed, this powerup will replenish a soldier's Health and Shield meters back to 100. You might want to save these rare powerups until the End Game, or consume it after a firefight that caused some major damage to your soldier.

A Chug Jug takes 15 seconds to consume, during which time your soldier can't use a weapon, build, or use their pickaxe, so or she is vulnerable to an attack. Make sure you're in a safe and secluded area when you consume a powerup like this one.

There are many buildings on the island that contain several levels. To reach the top, you can climb up the stairs inside, build a ramp outside from the ground to the roof, or if you have one, use a Launch Pad.

To use a Launch Pad, you'll often need to build one floor tile on the ground (wood was used here), and then place the Launch Pad directly on top of it. A Launch Pad is stored with your resources and does not require a slot in your soldier's backpack. Once built, it can be used as many times as you need it.

Jump onto the Launch Pad and your soldier will be catapulted into the air. To ensure a safe landing, the soldier's glider will activate. As your soldier is returning to the ground, use your directional controls to land at the desired location, which in this case was the roof of the building.

Traps also get stored with your resources. Once you find and collect them, they can be used to booby trap an area. Traps work best when they are hidden, so when an enemy stumbles on one, it activates. In most cases, a Trap will defeat that soldier. Within this building's doorway, there's a small area, in addition to a staircase.

Open the door and place a Trap on the inside side wall.

Once the Trap is set, close the door behind you and wait for a soldier to walk into this area and activate the Trap.

M

Mega Mansion (Secret Base)

From Lonely Lodge, for example, it's just a short drive in an ATK to the Mega Mansion. Just head southwest. It's located at map coordinates J5.5.

As you approach the mansion, head directly up to the front door.

At the front door, instead of opening the door and walking inside, use your pickaxe to smash into the ground. You'll drop down into the Mega Mansion's basement.

This is no ordinary basement, however. It's the location of a secret base. Search the entire base to discover several chests and other useful weapons, ammo, and loot items. When you're done exploring the secret base, go upstairs and explore the rest of the house, just like you would any other house. As always, watch and listen for enemies who might also be inside the Mega Mansion.

Within the main building, where the guest rooms once were, you'll discover at least two or three chests, along with weapons, ammo, and loot items lying out in the open (on the ground).

To reach the chest often found in this loft area, you'll need to build a ramp from the ground level.

Motel

Be sure to check the other guest rooms to find additional chests and goodies.

Located between map coordinates D2 and E2, you'll discover this derelict motel. It's not labeled on the map.

Located next to the motel is this broken-down house. You might want to take a moment and search it as well, especially if you're looking to expand your arsenal.

Movie Set

For more information about this movie set location, which is not listed on the map, see the description for Junk Junction in the "J" section.

When you visit this area, consider wearing the optional Moisty Merman outfit, for example, and maybe you'll land a guest starring role in the movie that's being shot here.

P

Paradise Palms

At the start of Season 5, what was once a swampland known as Moisty Mire was transformed into a vast desert. In the heart of this region is a small city, now known as Paradise Palms.

Paradise Palms has become one of the most popular points of interest on the island for these reasons:

- There are a bunch of buildings, houses, and other structures to explore.
- You'll often find Rifts here.
- This is one of the areas on the island where you're most apt to find an All Terrain Kart.
- Just outside of Paradise Palms, there are several smaller areas that are well worth visiting, including a Racetrack and a Western Village.

Just outside of Paradise Palms, near the Paradise billboard, is a stage coach exhibit. Here you'll often discover a chest. Because this is such as popular area, you always want to enter into Paradise Palms well-armed. Instead of landing right in the middle of this city area, land just outside, build up your arsenal, and then move it. If you're coming here from another point of interest, make sure you have at least one close-range, one mid-range, and one long-range weapon, along with plenty of ammo, so you can defend yourself or launch attacks in any type of situation you encounter.

As you enter the city, just past the billboard, you'll see this truck. Inside it, there's almost always a chest. Just beyond the truck, an ATK is often parked in front of the hotel.

Inside the car dealership is another two-story building you can explore. The main attractions here, however, are the vehicles parked in front. Smash them with your pickaxe to harvest some metal.

The hotel that's located near the center of Paradise Palms is the tallest building in the region. If you climb to the top, you'll be able to shoot down at your enemies below and have the tactical height advantage (unless someone builds a ramp or structure that goes up higher). Inside the hotel and within the swimming pool area outside, you'll discover multiple chests, along with weapons, ammo, loot items, and resource icons lying out on the ground. The trick is to be the first soldier to reach the hotel, so you can pick it clean of everything of value, load up your arsenal, and take your place high up.

On the roof of the hotel, you'll typically find a chest, but also have a great view of Paradise Palms. Use this to your advantage, and attack enemies below.

The gas station is one of the other buildings located in Paradise Palms. It's no different from the gas stations located in other parts of the island. Inside or on the roof, you'll often find useful items lying on the ground. Next to the gas station is a bus stop. There are several of these bus stops throughout the island. Inside many of them, you'll typically find weapons, ammo, and loot items lying on the ground.

As you walk, run, or drive an ATK around Paradise Palms, you'll discover a cluster of single-family houses. Each of these contains useful items to grab and perfect locations for taking part in close range firefights with enemies. Each house has many rooms. As always, be sure to check the attic, basement, and/or garage, when available, since these are the places you're most apt to discover chests.

Each house on the island may look different, but inside, they should all be searched and explored the same way. Enter one room at a time, consider setting Traps or Remote Explosives to defeat your enemies, and be prepared to engage in close-range firefights. Listen carefully for the sound of chests that may be nearby, but that you can't see.

While inside each house within Paradise Palms (or anywhere on the island for that matter), don't forget you can smash furniture, appliances, and other objects to harvest resources. Listen carefully for your enemy's footsteps or movements. This is the best way to determine if other soldiers are also lurking within the house.

Located just outside of Paradise Palms is a large gray building with a junk yard in the back. If you choose to enter into this area, treat it just like Junk Junction.

If you stay on ground level in the junkyard area, you become an easy target for soldiers hiding above you.

Try to stay higher up, and avoid the maze-like area created by the piles of junk vehicles. One benefit to this is that you'll often find chests and other goodies on top of the car piles.

As you walk, run, or drive out of Paradise Palms along the paved road, you'll come across these giant dinosaur exhibits. Sometimes (but not always), if you smash the dinos, a chest may be revealed. However, most of the time, smashing them simply generates extra resources.

When you come across this police car (and sometimes an empty ATK), take a left and go off-roading. You'll discover the small Western Town, which has its own collection of buildings and structures. On the island map, you'll find it at coordinates H9.5.

One of the more fun places you'll discover in Paradise Palms is this basketball court. There are several of them on the island. Before the match, if you placed the Basketball emote into your soldier's Emotes menu, you'll be able to play some hoops. When you reach this area, access your soldier's Emotes menu and select the Basketball.

Move around the directional controls and position your soldier just right, and he or she will be able to toss the basketball into the basket.

Pleasant Park

Located around map coordinates C3.5, this is another of the islands suburban areas. Here you'll find a cluster of single-family homes, a gas station, and a soccer field.

As you are learning to use a sniper rifle with a scope, aim at a non-moving object, such as a chest, that you know an enemy will soon approach. Then, as soon as the enemy walks into your line of fire and you see them within the scope, start shooting. Make sure your soldier is well protected behind a solid object or within a metal fortress in case you miss the shot and the enemy shoots back.

Treat the houses in this area just like any other houses you encounter on the island, keeping in mind that some will offer a better collection of chests, weapons, ammo, loot items, and resource icons than others.

The soccer field is an open area. There's often a chest in the middle of it. If you attempt to reach the chest and there are enemies in the area, they'll shoot at you, and you won't have anything to crouch behind for protection, unless you build something quickly. If you attempt to reach this chest, run (don't walk) in a zig-zag pattern and keep jumping to make your soldier a more difficult target to hit. When you reach the chest, build walls around it, so you'll be protected as you open the chest and collect its contents.

This structure in the center of town offers a great view of the entire region if you climb to the roof by building a ramp. On top of the roof, consider building a 1x1 fortress, so you'll be up higher than most of your enemies (or at least as high as the roof of any nearby house).

ATKs are often parked outside of a few homes within Pleasant Park. Sometimes they are parked inside a house's garage. Instead of hopping into an ATK and driving away, consider boobytrapping it with Remote Explosives. Once you do this and you see the blue lights from the explosives flashing, hide nearby and wait for an enemy soldier to approach the ATK. When they get into the vehicle, detonate the Remote Explosives, and make them go boom!

Each Building Tile Has Its Own Strength

When you're learning to build in *Fortnite: Battle Royale*, experiment with different structure designs, and develop the skillset needed to be able to build very quickly. If the Playground game play mode is currently offered (it's added and removed from the game periodically), this is the perfect place to practice building.

There are four shapes of building tiles—vertical wall tiles, horizontal floor/ceiling tiles, ramp/stair tiles, and pyramid-shaped tiles. Once you enter into Building mode, first choose your building material. Next, choose where you want to build. Finally, one at a time, select which building tile you want to use.

Each tile has an HP level that determines how much damage it can withstand before collapsing or being destroyed. During the building process, a tile's HP increases gradually. Wood is the fastest to build with, while working with stone is slightly slower. Metal takes the longest to build with but offers the most protection.

Each tile costs 10 of the selected resource to build. Remember, when you're in Building mode, you can't use a weapon. You'll definitely need to practice quickly switching between Combat mode and Building mode.

Here's a list of the HP strength offered by each tile type once it's fully built. Keep in mind, this information periodically changes when Epic Games tweaks this aspect of the game.

TILE SHAPE	WOOD	STONE	METAL
Horizontal Floor/ Ceiling Tile	140 HP	280 HP	460 HP
Vertical Wall Tile	150 HP	300 HP	500 HP
Ramp/Stairs Tile	140 HP	280 HP	460 HP
Pyramid-Shaped Tile	140 HP	280 HP	460 HP

When you go into Edit mode to alter a tile—to add a door or window, for example—the defensive strength of that tile changes. Each tile has its own HP meter which is displayed when you face the tile.

The trick to becoming a highly skilled builder is speed. Achieving speed takes practice! In order to build in *Fortnite: Battle Royale*, you must first collect or harvest resources (wood, stone, and metal).

Learn to Quickly Build "1x1" Fortresses

A 1x1 fortress is simply four walls around you, with a ramp in the center. It goes up multiple levels. Using wood allows you to build with the greatest speed, but using metal offers the greatest protection. Keep practicing until you're able to build this type of fortress very quickly.

Here's how to build a 1x1 fortress:

First build one floor tile if the ground is uneven. In this case, the 1x1 fortress is being built on the roof of an existing structure, so the floor tile was placed on the existing structure's roof.

Next, build four vertical walls so they surround you.

In the center of the structure, build a ramp. As the ramp is being constructed, jump on it. You've now built one level of a 1x1 fortress.

Repeat these steps until the fortress has reached the desired height.

At the top, consider adding pyramid-shaped roof pieces around the top for added protection when you peek out. However, if you need protection from above as well, add a flat roof and then a pyramid-shaped roof piece directly over your head. This 1x1 fortress is made of metal. It's three levels tall.

Learning to edit quickly, to add windows, doors, and other customizations to a structure you've built, is an important skill to master. It takes practice to be able to edit structures at lightning-fast speed. To begin editing, face a tile and press the Edit button on your controller or keyboard.

When you're editing a wall tile, choose which of the nine squares you want to remove.

Selecting and then removing one square creates a window. After selecting the tile, press the Confirm button to create the window, or select additional tiles to remove, and then use the Confirm command.

Selecting two squares (one on top of the other) creates a door. Removing two squares next to each other creates an extra wide window.

Any soldier can open and close a door that's been added to a structure.

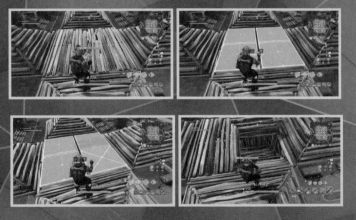

It's also possible to create a hole in the floor or ceiling of a structure you've built, so that it's easy for your soldier to travel up or down between levels. Start with a solid floor tile. It can be made of wood, stone, or metal.

Enter into Edit mode while facing a ground or ceiling tile.

Select one of the squares to remove.

Press the Confirm button to create the hole (in this case, on the floor tile).

To help ensure an enemy soldier won't follow you into your own fortress, consider adding a Trap to the wall or ceiling on the first level. Once the Trap is activated, when an enemy enters through the door, the Trap will inflict major injury or cause them to be eliminated from the match.

Shown here is the completed 1x1 fortress, with pyramid-shaped tiles around the roof, and a door on the bottom level. As you can see, it was built directly on top of an already existing structure in the center of Pleasant Park.

This is the view from the top of the 1x1 fortress. The soldier can use a Rocket Launcher (shown), Grenade Launcher, Guided Missile Launcher, or a Sniper Rifle, for example, to shoot at enemies in the distance as they come out of a house or are traveling out in the open.

Once you've climbed into an ATK, practice driving by racing around the track. If you pull up in front of this starting line, you can time how long it takes to complete a lap. If you're playing in Duos, Squads, 50 v 50, or Playground mode (shown here), for example, you can challenge your partner, squad mates, or online friends to a race. As you race around the track, watch out for enemies that may try to shoot at your ATK.

R

Racetrack

Located near map coordinates J6.5, one of the areas you'll discover in the desert is a racetrack. There are three main buildings surrounding the track, including a garage and an area for spectators. This is one of the areas on the island where you're guaranteed to find an All Terrain Kart (ATK), assuming you're one of the first soldiers to visit the area during a match.

Be sure to explore each of the buildings for useful items, while looking out for enemies.

From the rooftop of any building that surrounds the track, you're able to snipe at ATKs as they pass by. Any type of projectile explosive weapon will blow up the ATK and its passengers. Trying to shoot at a driver or passenger using a Sniper Rifle if the ATK is moving will defiantly be a challenge, however. From this location, a mid-to-long-range gun with a rapid-fire feature will work well for shooting at a moving ATK.

This is one of the buildings that surround the race track. In the garage bays, you'll typically find one or more parked ATKs.

Random Structures

Throughout the island, there are many random structures. You'll encounter many of them as you travel between points of interest. When you come across one of these structures, search inside to find weapons, ammo, loot items, and occasionally chests. While inside, consider smashing objects to harvest resources. When you look closely at the loft area of this small hut, can you spot the chest's glow from the outside? Build a ramp to reach it quickly.

When you come across a home anywhere on the island that has a cellar door on the outside, approach it, smash it open with your pickaxe, and then go downstairs into the basement. It's within these basements that you'll often find a chest.

Scattered randomly throughout the island are single-family homes. Some are broken down. Others are still intact. Regardless of their condition, if you search these stand-alone structures, you'll often find weapons, ammo, loot items, and resources to grab or harvest.

Each time Epic Games releases a game update (patch), you'll likely discover new, unlabeled areas and structures on the map, as well as new roads and paths you can follow as you travel between points of interest.

Explore the homes in Retail Row just as you would any others on the island. It's within the homes in this area that you'll discover the best collection of weapons, ammo, loot items, resource icons, and sometimes chests. The restaurants and shops offer a place to engage in close-range firefights, hide, or collect items lying on the ground or that are found within chests.

Retail Row

You'll find this point of interest labeled on the island map, near coordinates H6. This area contains a bunch of restaurants and shops, along with several single-family homes.

This multi-level business offers many places to explore. In the food aisle, you might stumble upon a chest, for example.

Sometimes, you'll spot a chest on the top of the water tower that's located near the edge of Retail Row. However, if there is a chest on top and you try smashing the tower, the chest will disappear. Build a ramp to the top, or land on the top of the tower after leaping from the Battle Bus. If you have a Launch Pad or Bouncer Pad, these items can also help you travel from ground level to the top of the water tower. Smashing the tower with your pickaxe will generate metal.

When you're traveling on ground level between buildings, you may need to duck behind a vehicle for protection if you're getting shot at. Another option is to quickly build a vertical wall tile with a ramp tile right behind it. When it's made of metal, this is the perfect, easy-to-build structure to hide behind.

Risky Reels

This drive-in movie theater is located at map coordinates H2. Just outside the theater area are a few stand-alone houses. Anytime you're visiting an area on the outskirts of the island, you often can't spend too much time exploring, or you'll get engulfed by the expanding and moving storm.

Here you can see one of the buildings located at the drive-in movie theater. Inside you'll likely find useful items. If you climb to the upper-level or the roof, use the higher-up position as a place to snipe at enemies below.

RV Parks & Campgrounds

If you're driving an ATK into this area, pull into a parking spot, and then search the surrounding trucks for chests. As always, you can hide behind cars and use them for cover if you're getting shot at, or smash them to harvest metal.

One of the RV parks you'll discover that's not labeled on the map is located at map coordinates I5.5.

If there are enemies in the area, stay on top of the RVs or surrounding structures in order to maintain the all-important tactical height advantage. However, if you know the area is clear, check the ground level for items, weapons, and ammo you can grab.

This long building that's next to a playground contains a bunch of picnic tables. More importantly, there are typically two chests to be found in here, along with items, weapons, and ammo lying out in the open.

Smashing the RVs with your pickaxe is an ideal way to harvest a lot of metal, which will definitely come in handy during the End Game, when you need to build. Of course, you can also exchange bundles of metal in Vending Machines to enhance your arsenal with powerful weapons or loot items.

S

Salty Springs

Like Pleasant Park, Salty Springs is another suburban area of the island that contains a few single-family homes. You'll find this area at map coordinates F7. Salty Springs is not too popular, compared to Tilted Towers or Paradise Palms, for example, but you still might run into enemy soldiers wanting to challenge you to a firefight. Be prepared!

Located just outside of Salty Springs is this wooden tower. Between the ground level and the top, if you take the stairs up, you're bound to come across at least one or two chests.

Shifty Shafts

This is the island's underground mining facility. Above ground, there are a few buildings and structures to explore. However, you also want to go below ground, into the tunnels, to find more chests and other useful items.

There are several entrances and exits to the underground tunnels. Once you're below ground, however, the tunnels follow a maze-like pattern with lots or twists and turns.

Since you can't see around sharp turns, and enemies could be hiding anywhere and waiting to attack, always proceed through these tunnels with your weapon drawn. It's best to use a close-to-mid-range weapon, such as a pistol or a shotgun in this area.

As you're exploring the mine tunnels, listen carefully for the sound of chests, and look for their glow behind the wooden planks.

When you notice the glow of a chest behind a wall, use your pickaxe to smash the wall. A few direct shots with any gun will also destroy the wall, or you could also use an explosive weapon, such as a Grenade, Clinger, or Remote Explosive to destroy it.

Once you reveal the chest, make sure the area is clear of enemies, and then open the chest to collect what's inside.

Snobby Shores

This is an upscale community on the island that's comprised of several large homes and mansions. It's located on the outskirts of the island, at map coordinates A5. If you plan to travel out of your way to visit Snobby Shores and explore the homes here, first check the location of the storm and where it'll be expanding and moving to next. Don't get caught in the storm!

Next to the guard house of one mansion, you'll often find at least one ATK parked outside, along with a Vending Machine. If you need a place to hide from enemies, inside this brick guard house (or one like it found elsewhere on the island) will do the trick.

Each mansion and home within Snobby Shores looks a bit different, but all contain multiple levels, each with a handful of rooms. Be prepared to engage in close-range combat if enemies are searching the same house as you are.

T

Tilted Towers

To practice your aim when using a sniper rifle (with a scope), from far away, target street signs and other smaller, non-moving, targets. Keep moving farther away from your target as you work on improving your aim.

Tilted Towers (located near map coordinates D5.5) is definitely one of the most popular points of interest on the island. If you visit here, you're guaranteed to encounter enemies—often lots of enemies. Your best bet here is to stay high up and avoid ground level as much as possible. If you need to travel between buildings, consider going to the roof of one building and then building a bridge to the next one.

Instead of landing in Tilted Towers after exiting the Battle Bus, consider landing in the outskirts of this city and building up your arsenal. There's a hill located just outside of Tilted Towers. On the top of the hill is this small hut. In the loft area of the hut, you'll often find a chest. Stock up on some guns and ammo, and then slide down the cliff (don't jump) to enter Tilted Towers.

One of the main attractions in Tilted Towers is the Clock Tower. If you land on the top of the Clock Tower and smash your way down, you'll discover at least three chests, as well as some other weapons and items. However, if you're not the first soldier to land here, avoid the Clock Tower, or you'll get shot at.

Be sure to check in the back of trucks for chests and other items. You can also hide in a truck to avoid enemy fire or wait inside to ambush an enemy.

If you get your hands on a Sniper Rifle, go to the roof of a building next to the Clock Tower and wait for enemy soldiers to land on or approach it . . . then shoot 'em!

Use a Grenade Launcher (shown), Rocket Launcher, or Guided Missile Launcher to shoot at enemies in other buildings. When you do this, you'll destroy a large part of the building, and injure (or defeat) anyone inside unless they quickly take cover to avoid the explosion.

When you're inside one building (on a top floor or near the roof), use a sniper rifle to spot enemy soldiers in neighboring buildings and shoot at them through the window.

pyramid was built in the center of this area. You'll discover chests and other useful items Inside and around the pyramid, but watch out for enemies. There are many small chambers where someone can hide and ambush you. As you can see by looking at the top of the pyramid, Tomatohead still reigns here.

A Grappler is a loot item that allows you to quickly reach high-up areas or swing from tall objects like Spider-Man. When aiming this tool, as long as you see a round targeting icon over your intended target, the Grappler will work. As soon as you shoot it, your soldier will be quickly drawn to the target location.

If your soldier is the first to arrive here, you'll discover weapons, ammo, and loot items lying on the ground, out in the open, and within many of the stone chambers.

Tomato Temple

Behind and below the pyramid there are additional ancient stone structures to explore, including below this modern house.

Late in Season 5, Tomato Tower was transformed into Tomato Temple. A large stone

You can enter or exit the Tomato Town area by traveling through this tunnel. If you're driving an ATK, avoid the obstacles in your path.

Several of these big-headed stone statues can be found around the island, including just out-side of Tomato Town. When you find one, you'll likely find one or maybe two chests by the base of the statue. Use your pickaxe to smash the statue to harvest stone.

V

Viking Village

The Viking Village was added to the island at the start of Season 5. You'll find it at the very top of a large mountain, near map coordinates B5.5. This area contains a bunch of buildings, each of which offers a different collection of chests, weapons, ammo, loot items, and resource icons. This has become a popular place to visit on the island, so be prepared to engage enemy soldiers in close- to mid-range firefights.

If you don't land on top of this mountain after leaping from the Battle Bus, there's a windy road that leads up to this area.

The "must see" attraction in this area is the massive Viking ship. Climb into the ship and be sure to explore its hull (below the top deck).

All hands on deck! There's a firefight about to break out on the Viking ship. Are you well armed and ready to defend yourself?

From the top deck of the ship, smash your way down to enter into the ship's hull. Watch for the glow of a chest if you're the first soldier to reach this area.

One of the buildings near the ship contains a loft area. You'll need to build a ramp to reach it. In this upper-level, you'll likely stumble upon a chest.

W

Wailing Woods

This area of the island contains a dense forest. Smashing each of the tall and thick trees here will generate a lot of wood. You'll find this forest around map coordinates I3.5.

In the center of Wailing Woods is a hedge maze, and in the center of that is a wooden tower. Climb the tower and go into the wooden hut to collect items from a chest that's often there, plus collect items lying on the ground within the hut and on the steps leading up to it.

If you stay on ground level within the hedge maze, an enemy soldier could sneak up on you and attack. Be ready to defend yourself with a close-range weapon. A better strategy is to climb on top of the hedges and look for enemies below you. This is another situation where having a height advantage will work in your favor.

In the middle of the woods, you'll encounter this metal entrance to an underground bunker. During Season 5, it was not possible to open this door and enter the bunker. Why this bunker entrance was placed here, and what's inside, is a mystery that'll likely be solved during Season 6 (or beyond).

Scattered randomly on the ground in wooded areas on the island, look for blue mushrooms. When you encounter one, approach it and press the Consume button on your controller (or keyboard/mouse). When you consume a mushroom, your soldier's Shield meter will increase by 5 points (up to 100). In other areas, look for red Apples under trees. When you consumer an Apple, your soldier's Health meter will increase by 5 points (up to 100). Unlike other health and shield powerups, you can't pick up and carry Mushrooms or Apples in your backpack. You need to consume them as soon as you find them.

What You Should Know About Health and Shield Powerups

Scattered randomly throughout the island, and found out in the open, you'll come across several different types of health and shield powerup items. These are used to replenish your Health and/or Shield meter. On most gaming systems, a soldier's Health meter (displayed as a green bar) can be found at the bottom-center of the screen. A soldier's Shield meter (displayed as a blue bar when active) is displayed directly above it.

You'll also often find health and shield powerup items within chests, Supply Drops, and Loot Llamas. When you defeat an enemy, if that soldier was carrying any of these items, they'll become yours to grab if you want them. Most take up a slot within your soldier's backpack, although some get stored with your resources and become accessible from within Build mode. In most cases, you can carry multiples of the same item within the same backpack slot.

Each item takes a different amount of time to consume or use, during which time your soldier will be vulnerable to attack. Before consuming or using a health or shield powerup, make sure your soldier is in a safe location. At the start of a match, your soldier's Health meter will be maxed out at 100 HP. Each time he or she gets injured, it will diminish. When a soldier's Health meter reaches zero, he or she is immediately eliminated from the match.

Meanwhile, at the start of a match, your soldier's Shield meter will be at zero. By consuming or using a shield-related powerup, you will activate his or her shields and boost them to a maximum of 100. Shields will help to protect a soldier from enemy weapons and explosions, but not from the storm or from falls. Before engaging in any type of firefight or battle, it's always best to boost your soldier's Health and Shield meter as high as possible (up to 100).

LOOT ITEM NAME	DESCRIPTION	REPLENISHES HEALTH	REPLENISHES SHIELDS	TIME REQUIRED TO USE OR CONSUME IT
Apples	Grab and consume an Apple right when and where you find it. It will replenish 5 points to your soldier's Health meter.	Yes	No	Almost Instant
Bandages	Boost your soldier's Health meter by 15 points each time you use Bandages.	Yes	No	4 Seconds
Chug Jug	Replenish your soldier's Health meter and Shield meter to 100.	Yes	Yes	15 Seconds
Cozy Campfire	For each second a soldier stands next to the flame, his or her health will increase by 2 points. The flame lasts 25 seconds.	Yes	No	25 Seconds
Med Kit	Replenish your soldier's Health meter back to 100.	Yes	No	10 Seconds
Mushrooms	Replenish your soldier's Shield meter by 5 points.	No	Yes	Almost instant
Shield Potion	Replenish your soldier's Shield meter by 50 points.	No	Yes	5 Seconds
Slurp Juice	Replenish your soldier's Health meter *and* Shield meter by 25 points.	Yes	Yes	2 Seconds to consume, and then up to 25 Seconds to fully utilize
Small Shield Potion	Replenish your soldier's Shield meter by 25 points.	No	Yes	2 Seconds

Keep in mind, as new *Fortnite: Battle Royale* game updates are released by Epic Games, new health and shield powerup items are sometimes introduced, while others are removed from the game, or their capabilities are somehow altered.

When a weapon or item's capabilities are diminished within the game, this is referred to as being "nerfed." When something is removed from the game altogether, this is referred to as being "vaulted." Anything that Epic Games chooses to vault could be reintroduced into the game at any time in the future.

Choose the Ideal Landing Location

If you're looking for a secluded place to land after leaping from the Battle Bus, and you want to quickly build up your arsenal before going face-to-face against any enemies, one ideal landing location is this house with a wooden tower on its roof. It's located just outside of Wailing Woods, between map coordinates I2.5 and J2.5. By searching the wooden tower as well as the house and its garage, you're apt to find two or three chests, plus plenty of other worthwhile goodies.

You can build your arsenal faster by visiting this house than by visiting the hedge maze within nearby Wailing Woods, but you're less apt to encounter enemies in or near the house. In the garage of this house, there's often an empty ATK that's waiting for a driver.

If you want to hop into the driver's seat of an ATK almost immediately upon reaching the island (after leaping from the Battle Bus), the best places to land include Lazy Links or Paradise Palms. However, you'll very likely encounter enemies within seconds after touching ground.

When you watch live streams (on YouTube or Twitch.tv) of the top-ranked *Fortnite: Battle Royale* players, one strategy you'll often see them implement is choosing a very remote place to land once their soldier jumps from the Battle Bus. They'll choose a landing location they know offers multiple chests that can be found and opened within moments of landing.

After you've collected an initial arsenal of weapons and loot items, instead of spending time visiting the island's various points of interest, determine where the storm is headed (by looking at the map), and avoid enemy soldiers early on in a match by staying exclusively in the outskirts of popular island locations.

By staying out of the popular points of interest early in the match, you'll likely encounter only a few enemy soldiers. You can choose to fight them, or often avoid them altogether to ensure your soldier will stay alive longer. As the storm continues to expand, focus on staying within the eye of the storm (the circle), while building up your arsenal and resource collection before the circle gets really small, and you're forced to fight the remaining enemy soldiers during the End Game.

Among the many other potential landing sites that allow you to quickly grab weapons, ammo, and loot items, but often avoid immediate enemy contact, includes a cluster of homes and buildings near map coordinates D8, and the tall wooden tower located between map coordinates I4.5 and J4.5 (outside of Lonely Lodge). Up to three chests can often be found within this tower.

If you take a more aggressive approach and land in the heart of a point of interest, like Tilted Towers, Paradise Palms, or Lazy Links, you will definitely encounter enemies, often within the first few seconds after landing. Initially, you'll only be armed with a pickaxe, which is no match for any type of gun or explosive.

Anytime another soldier has beaten you to your landing location, chances are he or she will already be armed with a weapon and you'll be virtually defenseless. Unless you quickly find cover or a weapon, you will be eliminated from the match within seconds of landing.

Western Town

Located near map coordinates H9.5 is a small Western Town. It has two main entrances and exits if you follow the roads. Most of the structures in this area are one or two stories tall. Each contains a chest, or at least a good collection of weapons, ammo, loot items, and resource icons that'll be lying on the ground if you're the first soldier to reach them.

The inside of most structures within the Western Town contain furniture. Smash these items to collect resources, but also grab anything useful you find inside.

This town is less popular than Paradise Palms. Consider landing here to build up your arsenal and then traveling to Paradise Palms if you want to take part in firefights. If you spot an enemy, go to a roof to get the height advantage, and then shoot at them. Don't forget, using an explosive weapon, it's pretty easy to damage or destroy entire structures from a distance, and at the same time, injure anyone hiding within them.

Taking an ATK off-road is one of the most exciting things you can do in the desert area. There are plenty of hills, cliffs, and rough terrain areas you can drive over, under, and through.

If the ATK flips sideways, your soldier likely won't be injured. Some of the ATK's HP will get depleted, however. To fix the situation, you'll have to exit the vehicle and then press the Flip button on the controller (or keyboard/mouse) to get the ATK upright again.

When driving away from the desert area toward the West, you'll encounter this broken bridge. To cross it, you'll need to build some wooden floor tiles to fill in the bridge's gap before you can safely drive over it.

SECTION 4

FORTNITE: BATTLE ROYALE RESOURCES

On YouTube (www.youtube.com) or Twitch.TV (www.twitch.tv/directory/game/Fortnite), in the Search field, enter the search phrase "*Fortnite: Battle Royale*" to discover many game-related channels, live streams, and prerecorded videos that'll help you become a better player.

Also, be sure to check out these other online resources:

WEBSITE OR YOUTUBE CHANNEL NAME	DESCRIPTION	URL
Fandom's *Fortnite* Wiki	Discover the latest news and strategies related to *Fortnite: Battle Royale*.	http://fortnite.wikia.com/wiki/Fortnite_Wiki
FantasticalGamer	A popular YouTuber who publishes *Fortnite* tutorial videos.	www.youtube.com/user/FantasticalGamer
FBR Insider	The *Fortnite: Battle Royale Insider* website offers game-related news, tips, and strategy videos.	www.fortniteinsider.com
Fortnite Gamepedia Wiki	Read up-to-date descriptions of every weapon, loot item, and ammo type available within *Fortnite: Battle Royale.* This Wiki also maintains a comprehensive database of soldier outfits and related items released by Epic Games.	https://fortnite.gamepedia.com/Fortnite_Wiki
Fortnite Intel	An independent source of news related to *Fortnite: Battle Royale*.	www.fortniteintel.com
Fortnite Scout	Check your personal player stats, and analyze your performance using a bunch of colorful graphs and charts. Also check out the stats of other *Fortnite: Battle Royale* players.	www.fortnitescout.com
Fortnite Stats & Leaderboard	This is an independent website that allows you to view your own *Fortnite*-related stats or discover the stats from the best players in the world.	https://fortnitestats.com
Game Informer Magazine's *Fortnite* Coverage	Discover articles, reviews, and news about *Fortnite: Battle Royale* published by *Game Informer* magazine.	www.gameinformer.com/search/searchresults.aspx?q=Fortnite
GameSkinny Online Guides	A collection of topic-specific strategy guides related to *Fortnite*.	www.gameskinny.com/tag/fortnite-guides/

(Continued on next page)

GameSpot's *Fortnite* Coverage	Check out the news, reviews, and game coverage related to *Fortnite: Battle Royale* that's been published by GameSpot.	www.gamespot.com/fortnite
IGN Entertainment's *Fortnite* Coverage	Check out all IGN's past and current coverage of *Fortnite*.	www.ign.com/wikis/fortnite
Jason R. Rich's Website and Social Media Feeds	Share your *Fortnite: Battle Royale* game play strategies with this book's author and learn about his other books.	www.JasonRich.com www.FortniteGameBooks.com Twitter: @JasonRich7 Instagram: @JasonRich7
Microsoft's Xbox One *Fortnite* Website	Learn about and acquire *Fortnite: Battle Royale* if you're an Xbox One gamer.	www.microsoft.com/en-US/store/p/ Fortnite-Battle-Royalee/BT5P2X999VH2
MonsterDface YouTube and Twitch.tv Channels	Watch video tutorials and live game streams from an expert *Fortnite* player.	www.youtube.com/user/ MonsterdfaceLive www.Twitch.tv/MonsterDface
Ninja	Check out the live and recorded game streams from Ninja, one of the most highly skilled *Fortnite: Battle Royale* players in the world, on Twitch.tv and YouTube.	www.twitch.tv/ninja_fortnite_hyper www.youtube.com/user/NinjasHyper
Nomxs	A YouTube and Twitch.tv channel hosted by online personality Simon Britton (Nomxs). He too is one of *Fortnite*'s top-ranked players.	https://youtu.be/np-8cmsUZmc or www.twitch.tv/videos/259245155
Official Epic Games YouTube Channel for *Fortnite: Battle Royale*	The official *Fortnite: Battle Royale* YouTube channel.	www.youtube.com/user/epicfortnite
Turtle Beach Corp.	This is one of many companies that make great quality, wired or wireless (Bluetooth) gaming headsets that work with all gaming platforms.	www.turtlebeach.com

Your *Fortnite: Battle Royale* Adventure Continues . . .

Our driving tour of the island where *Fortnite: Battle Royale* takes place has come to an end. All Terrain Karts (ATKs) allow you to travel virtually anywhere on the island quickly. Throughout the island, you'll find an interconnected network of paved roadways and paths that run between the major points of interest. You can easily drive along these roads and paths, but you'll likely miss out on the experience of taking the ATK off-road and seeing what random structures and sights can be discovered.

When you follow the roads and paths, you're more likely to encounter enemies with projectile weapons who are waiting on nearby hills or mountains (or behind a large object) waiting for your ATK to pass by. As you approach, a surprise attack will be launched, and quick evasive maneuvers will be required if you have any hope of survival.

If you're the only soldier in your ATK, don't forget you can jump out of the vehicle at any time, with your weapon drawn, and begin firing almost instantly. When you have one or more passengers in your ATK, they can return fire as enemies attack. You can also attempt to run over enemies, but this typically won't cause enough damage to disable soldiers, unless they're unarmed to begin with.

As you'll quickly discover, the island is chock full of wonderous places to visit, so the more places you're able to visit during each match, the more fun you'll have playing *Fortnite: Battle Royale*'s various game play modes.

Whether you're experiencing a Solo, Duos, Squads, 50 v 50, or even the Playground mode, Epic Games is constantly releasing game updates (patches) that introduce new places to explore on the island, as well as new types of weapons and loot items that are guaranteed to keep things interesting during each and every match you experience.

If you're new to playing *Fortnite: Battle Royale*, don't expect to be able to defeat lots of enemies and achieve #1 Victory Royale right away. This is going to take a lot of practice! In the meantime, get to know the layout of the island, discovering how to use the various type of weapons and loot items, and use your creativity when visiting different types of terrain, so you can use your surroundings to your tactical advantage.

Remember, keep practicing and go into each match with the plan to have fun!